# Pretty Ugly

A Visual World of the Wonderfully Weird

# Preface

We've grown tired of perfection.

In a world filtered through algorithms and polished to a sanitised shine, something real and raw is breaking through. The artists gathered in this collection aren't interested in pleasing everyone. They're creating work that lives in that electric space where attraction and repulsion meet—a space we've come to call Pretty Ugly.

These pages showcase illustrations that grab you by the collar and demand your attention. Not because they're conventionally beautiful, but because they're honestly, unapologetically themselves. The creatures staring back at you from these pages aren't safely contained behind the glass of good taste. They're weird, they're uncomfortable, and they're absolutely mesmerising.

Gaetan Sahsah-(pp.084–091) describes "pretty ugly" as "the sweet spot where charm meets chaos." It's what happens when creators stop worrying about how things "should" look and instead embrace the freedom of honest expression. The results aren't always easy to digest, but they're impossible to forget.

The work collected here thrives in contradiction. Bright, candy-coloured palettes house unsettling characters. Meticulously crafted compositions feature deliberately awkward forms. These juxtapositions create a visual tension that keeps pulling you back for another look, making you question why you're drawn to something that simultaneously repels you.

As Gregory Jacobsen-(pp.098–113) puts it, "Finding attraction in repulsion" isn't just an artistic philosophy, but a more honest way of seeing the world. The artists featured here understand that beauty without strangeness feels empty, and perfection without personality feels dead. Their work pulses with life precisely because it embraces imperfection, oddity, and discomfort.

When you flip through these pages, get ready to be immersed in raw creative expression. Featured within this showcase are creatives who reject the pressure to smooth out their rough edges, and instead, they've discovered that those edges—those lumps, bumps, and uncomfortable bits—are exactly where the magic happens. As Chi Park-(pp.164–171) notes, "pretty ugly" emerges "when you embrace your imperfections, wild imaginations and personality just plainly with joy without worrying about how things should look."

This collection celebrates artists who aren't afraid to push beyond "pretty" into territory that challenges, unsettles, and transforms. Lumps-(pp.068–075) describes it as something that is "so wrong it loops back around to feeling right again." Their distortions and exaggerations aren't flaws, but instead deliberate choices that cut through the visual noise of an over-designed world.

In their deliberate ugliness lies an authenticity that polished commercial visuals can never achieve, Pretty Ugly sits as a reminder that true artistic expression often emerges not from following rules but from the courage to break them with conviction.

The journey through these pages won't always be comfortable. These illustrations won't just sit quietly in the background; they'll provoke, challenge, and sometimes even disturb. But in doing so, they offer something far more valuable than mere decoration: they offer a fresh perspective that stays with you long after you close the book.

Welcome to a visual world where weird isn't wrong—it's wonderful; where pretty and ugly aren't opposites, but partners in creative crime.

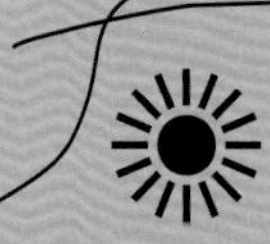

# Spotlight


01 pp.008–025 Gao Hang

02 pp.098–113 Gregory Jacobsen

03 pp.200–217 Rui Pu


# Showcase


pp.026–097, 114–199, 218–301

special feature
Spotlight

@gaohangart ☀ Gao Hang is a Chinese contemporary artist based in Houston. His vibrant, digital-inspired paintings draw on the rawness and absurdity of internet culture. Treating digital graphics as modern "found objects," he explores awkwardness and spectacle through a painterly lens, blending humour with critique. His process embraces unpredictability, mirroring the chaotic energy of online imagery.

# Q & A

Could you share a little bit about your background/journey so far with our readers? How has your creative expression evolved over the years until you arrived at your current aesthetic/artistic style and medium(s) you work with?

My journey as an artist has been shaped by years of self-reflection and exploration. I began by experimenting with traditional mediums, gradually transitioning to digital and airbrush techniques. Over time, I embraced hard-edged colour fields and low-poly aesthetics, inspired by digital culture and video games, which now define my style.

What role does your personal identity/lived experience or cultural background play in shaping your artistic vision?

My personal background and lived experience—particularly growing up in a Chinese family and navigating different cultural landscapes—deeply influence my artistic vision. I am constantly questioning authenticity, digital simulation, and the concept of reality through my works, reflecting both my personal struggles and observations of modern culture.

If your art could communicate one universal truth or idea about the human experience, what would it be?

The world is a simulation.

Could you walk us through your creative process or a typical day in the studio?

My creative process starts with immersing myself in the digital realm—exploring video games, glitch art, and 3D graphics. In the studio, I embrace unpredictability, using airbrush techniques to experiment with colour and form. I allow accidents to guide my work, creating an organic tension between structure and chaos.

Where do you typically find inspiration for your artistic concepts and outcomes? Do you encounter creative blocks often and if so, how do you overcome them?

Inspiration comes from the digital age, particularly early video games and digital aesthetics. When I encounter creative blocks, I revisit these influences—often engaging with online spaces or reworking existing ideas, allowing myself to break free from rigid expectations.

How important is experimentation to you? How do you embrace imperfections and use them in your favour?

Experimentation is central to my art. I embrace imperfections as part of the creative process, believing that accidents and imperfections can introduce unexpected beauty. These flaws often mirror the distortions in digital imagery, adding a sense of authenticity to my work.

What emotions or reactions do you hope to evoke in viewers who encounter your work? How do you approach criticism or misunderstandings, especially when challenging aesthetic norms?

I aim to evoke both attraction and discomfort in my viewers, as I explore the tension between the real and the simulated. I welcome criticism as an opportunity to refine my work, but remain grounded in my authenticity, even when challenging traditional norms.

How do you see the "pretty ugly" aesthetic evolving in the future, and what impact could it have on our world on a broader scale?

Artists have been exploring this idea through movements like "bad art", and we all know that bad art does not mean the art is bad. In that sense, I would say "pretty ugly" is also an experiment. We will see where it leads.

Why do you think society is increasingly drawn to unconventional aesthetics and what does it say about our culture?

But then again, hasn't it always been this way since the very beginning?

What advice would you give to emerging artists who want to break away from conventional beauty standards in their work? How can they stay truly authentic when surrounded by noise?

Read.

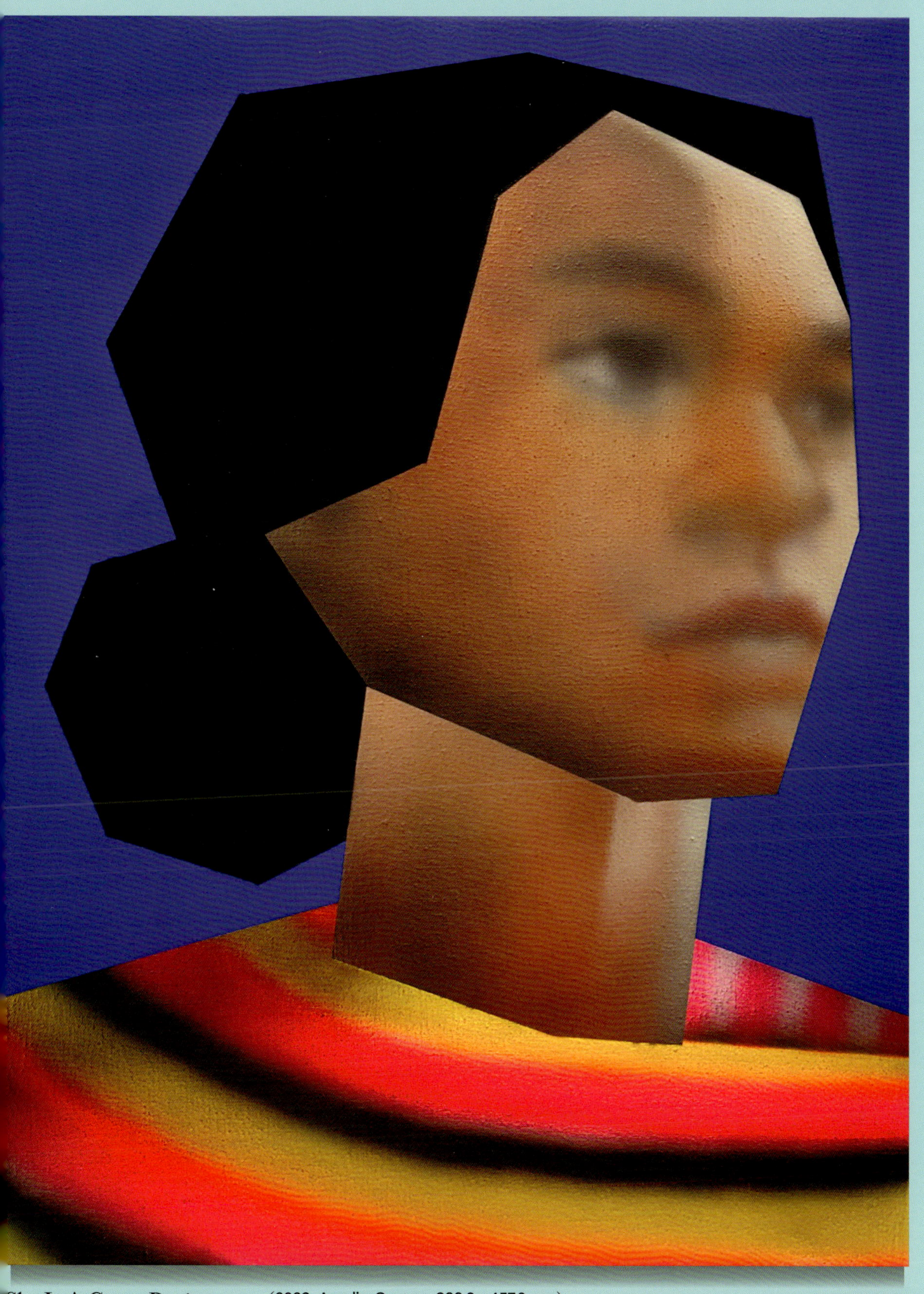

She Is A Game Designer__(2023_Acrylic, Canvas_609.6 x 457.2 mm).jpg

A Perfectly Beautiful Hand_(2021_Acrylic, Canvas_406.4 x 508 mm).jpg

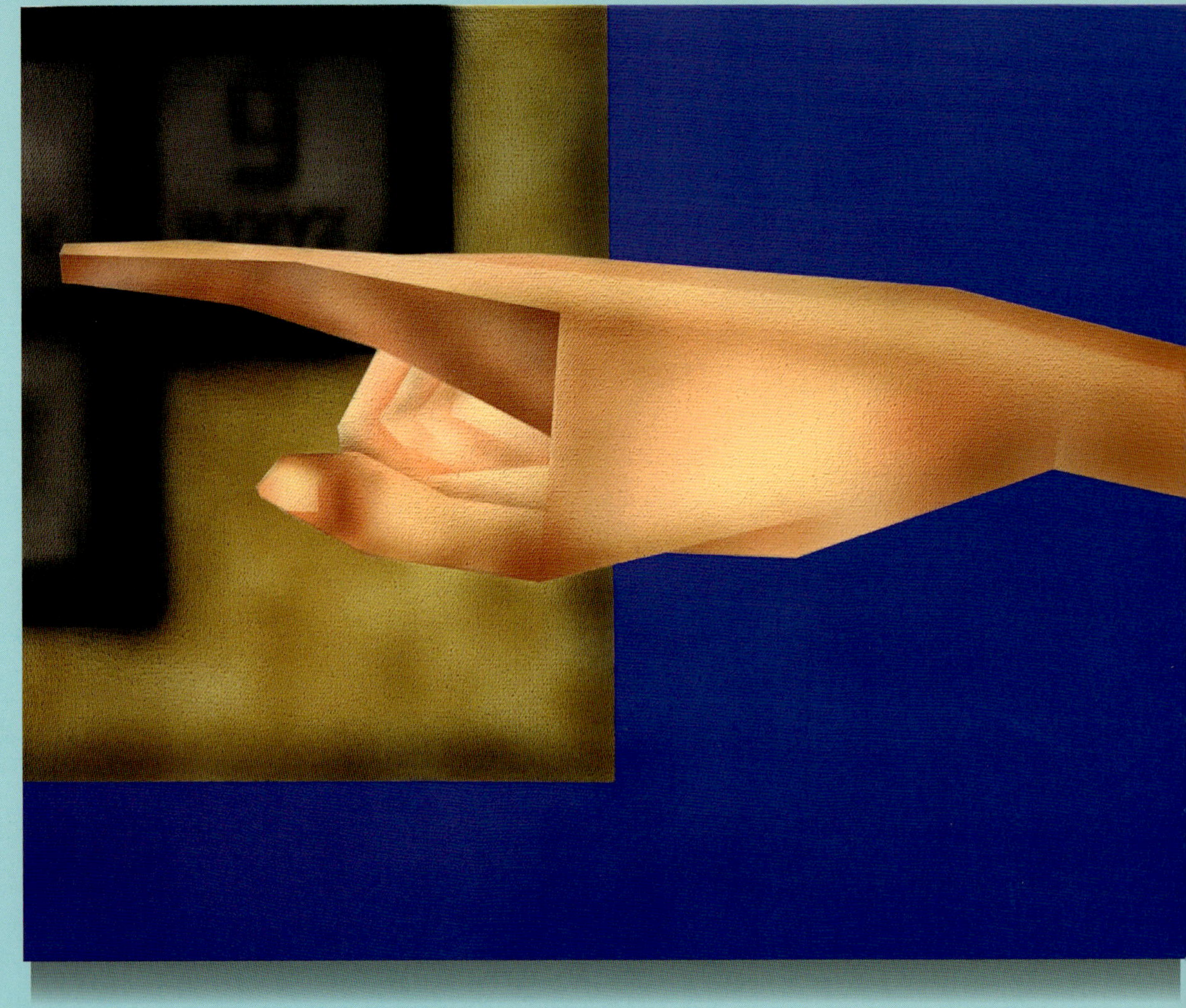

A Bigger Suck It_(2021_Acrylic, Canvas_1828.8 x 1524 mm).jpg

 Get My Wife's Face Out Of Your Painting_(2022_Acrylic, Canvas_609.6 x 457.2 mm).jpg

Your Wife's Best Friend_(2024_Acrylic, Canvas_609.6 x 508 mm).jpg

Your Children Are Protected_(2022_Acrylic, Canvas_1219.2 x 1219.2 mm).jpg

Mom Must Be So Proud Of Me_(2021_Acrylic, Canvas_1219.2 x 1219.2 mm).jpg

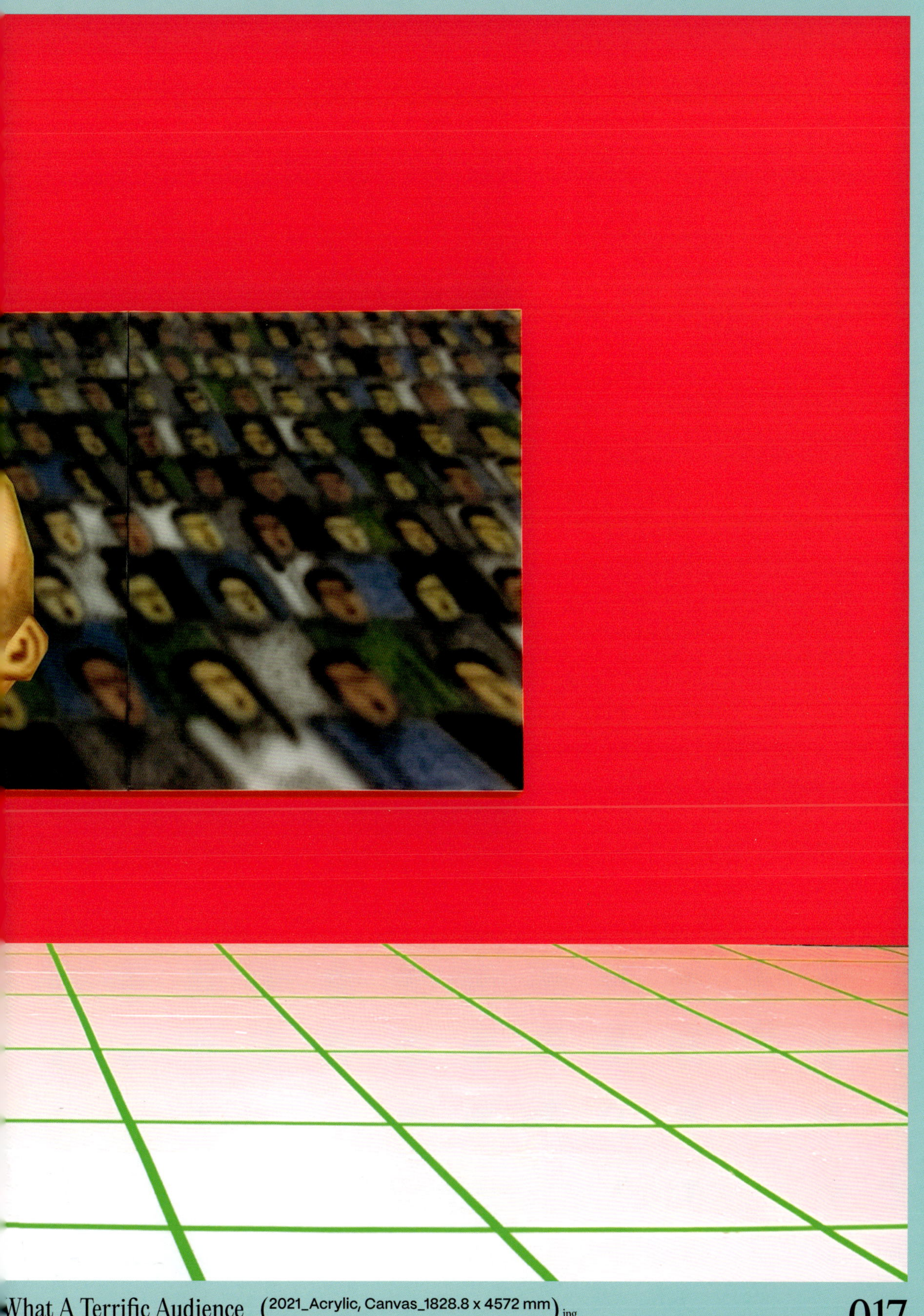

What A Terrific Audience_(2021_Acrylic, Canvas_1828.8 x 4572 mm).jpg

This Is A Goat_(2024_Acrylic, Canvas_762 x 1219.2 mm).jpg

Your Teammate_(2022_Acrylic, Canvas_1219.2 x 1524 mm).jpg

Your Teammate_(2022_Acrylic, Canvas_1219.2 x 1524 mm).jpg

Welcome Home_(2023_Acrylic, Canvas_1524 x 1828.8 mm).jpg

You See You Are Also Simulated Buddy_(2024_Acrylic, Canvas_609.6 x 508 mm).jpg

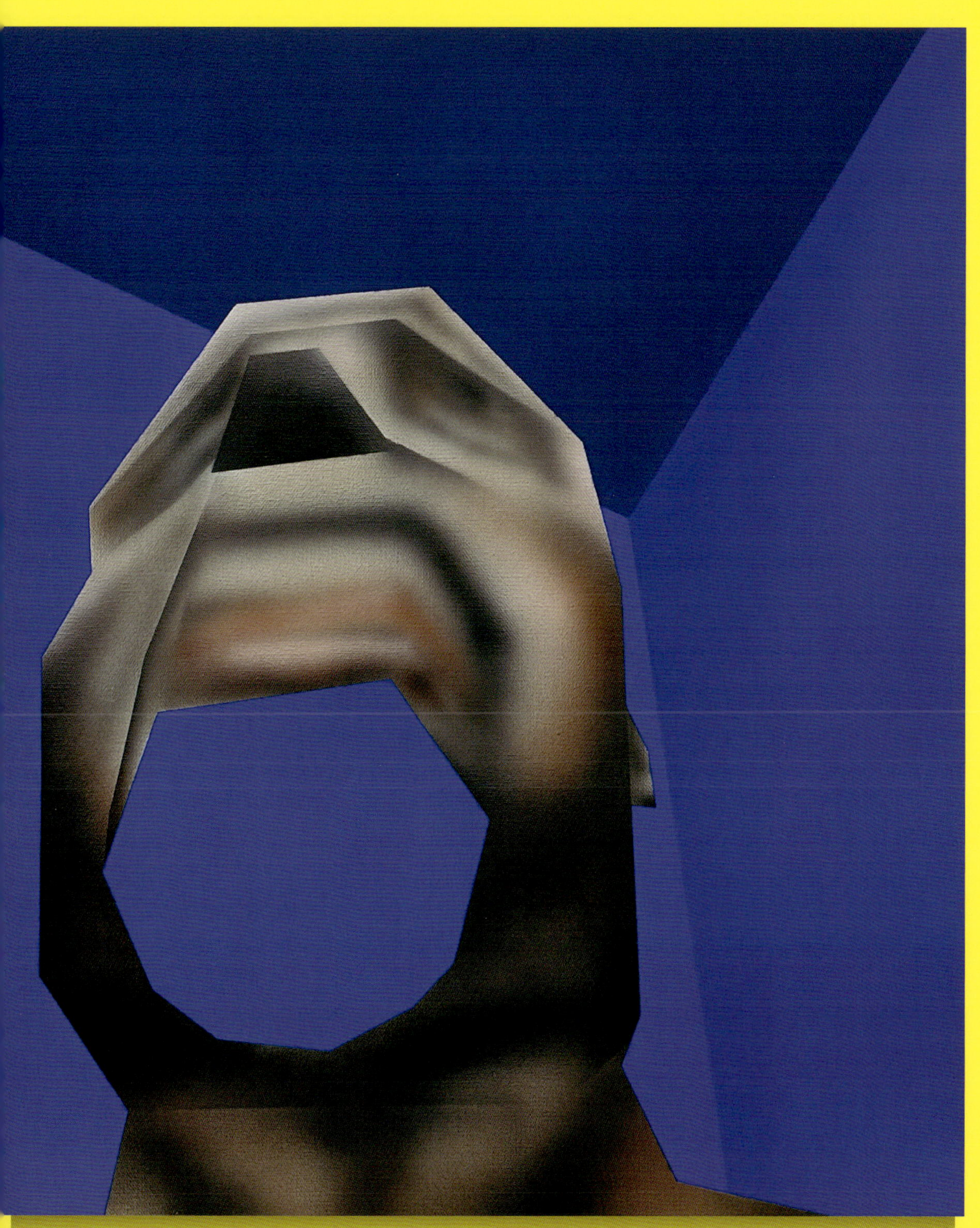

Guess My Ethnic Please_(2022_Acrylic, Canvas_1016 x 762 mm).jpg

Are You Stereotyping Me_(2022_Acrylic, Canvas_1016 x 762 mm).jpg

Everyone Else Totally Sucks_(2022_Acrylic, Canvas_609.6 x 1828.8 mm).jpg

"Beauty can be found all around us, even in the difficulties of life and in decay and things that are conventionally considered to be ugly."

Bijijoo

Bijijoo is a North Carolina-based artist and scientist whose layered paintings blend traditional and digital media. Drawing from backgrounds in biophysics and visual art, he explores the tension between chaos and form through automatic drawing. His surreal, often grotesque figures reflect themes of struggle, joy, and introspection—emerging from a process as intuitive as it is experimental.

Disguise_(2023_Oil, Acrylic, Pastel, Canvas_1600 x 1600 mm).jpg

Fish For Dinner_(2022_Oil, Acrylic, Canvas_1000 x 1000 mm).jpg

Music Practice_(2022_Oil, Acrylic, Canvas_1000 x 1000 mm).jpg

Meditation_(2022_Oil, Acrylic, Canvas_1000 x 1000 mm).jpg

Friends_(2023_Oil, Acrylic, Pastel, Canvas_1560 x 1560 mm).jpg

Oh My God_(2023_Oil, Acrylic, Canvas_1500 x 1500 mm).jpg

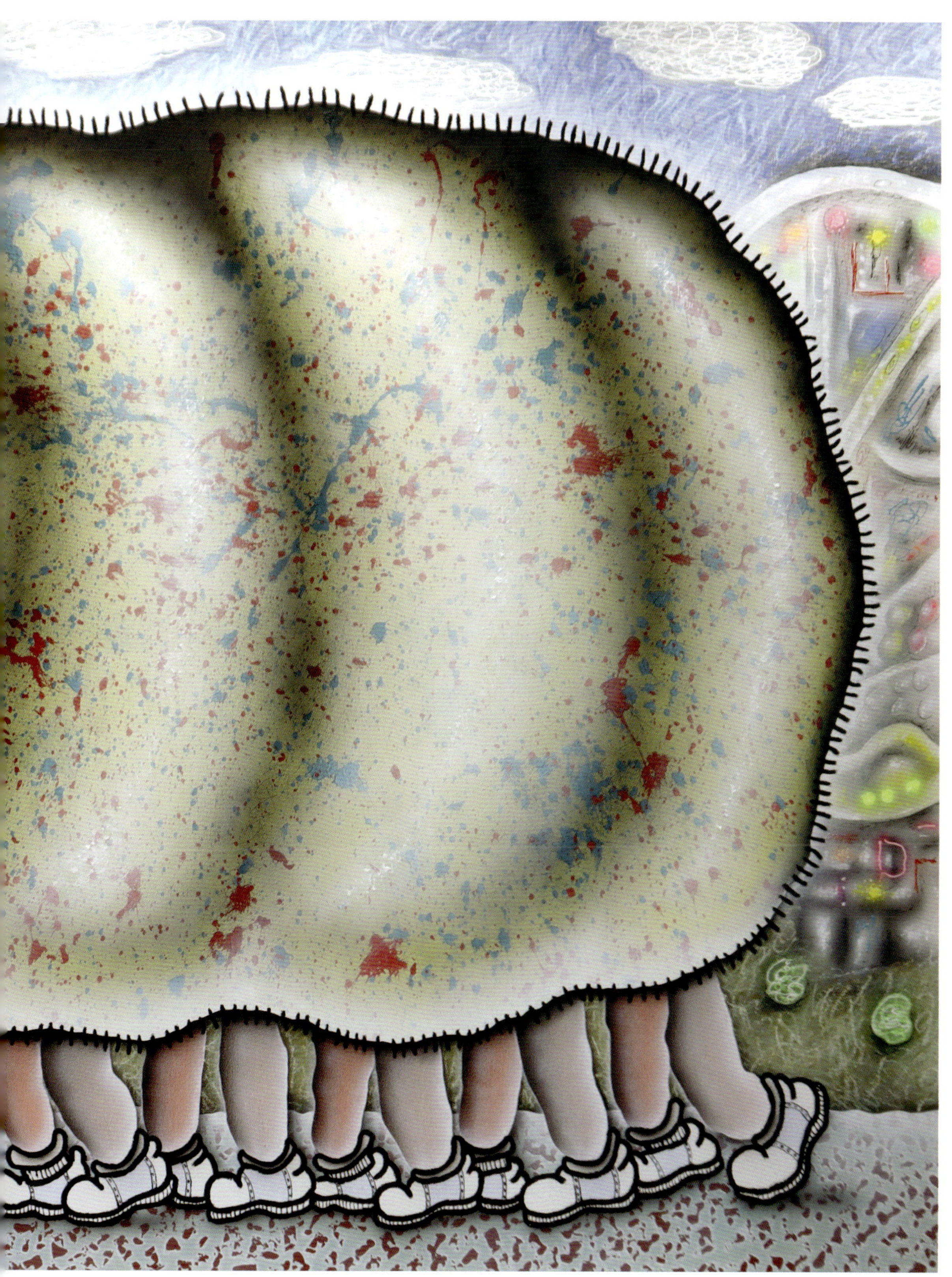

Wiggler_(2022_Oil, Acrylic, Canvas_1800 x 3000 mm).jpg

"'Pretty ugly' is my personal ethos! I like to challenge the idea of good taste, so I really enjoy the idea of making gleefully ugly work and being unapologetically garish."

Gary Card

Gary Card is a London-based artist, set designer, and illustrator known for his surreal, cartoon-infused worlds and sculptural works. Drawing inspiration from 80s/90s animation and global historical references, he uses everyday materials like tape and cardboard to build fantastical scenes. His playful yet raw approach reflects both his childhood and early fashion industry roots.

Woozy Winks_(2023_Oil, Acrylic, Canvas_1000 x 1200 mm).jpg

Boomer Groomer_(2023_Oil, Acrylic, Canvas_600 x 800 mm).jp

Giddy Whippet_(2023_Oil, Acrylic, Canvas_600 x 800 mm).jpg

Creepy 3some_(2022_Acrylic, Canvas_610 x 914 mm).jpg

Couple_(2022_Acrylic, Canvas_1219 x 1524 mm).jpg

Untitled (Boy II)_(2024_Oil, Canvas_700 x 300 mm).jpg

“For me, ‘pretty ugly’ celebrates the beauty in imperfection and contradictions. It’s about unconventional, unique beauty that challenges norms, resonates deeply, and shows that true beauty lies in expression, not perfection.”

Sophie Kuhn

Sophie Kuhn is a freelance artist and illustrator based in Karlsruhe. She creates vibrant, contrasting works featuring often grumpy, mostly female characters. Reflecting on the mood of her characters, she notes that they may not be upset, but simply weary of society's expectations for women to always smile and appear pleasant.

Mood_(2023_Digital_210 x 297 mm).jpg

Paperwork Panic_(2023_Digital_210 x 297 mm).jpg

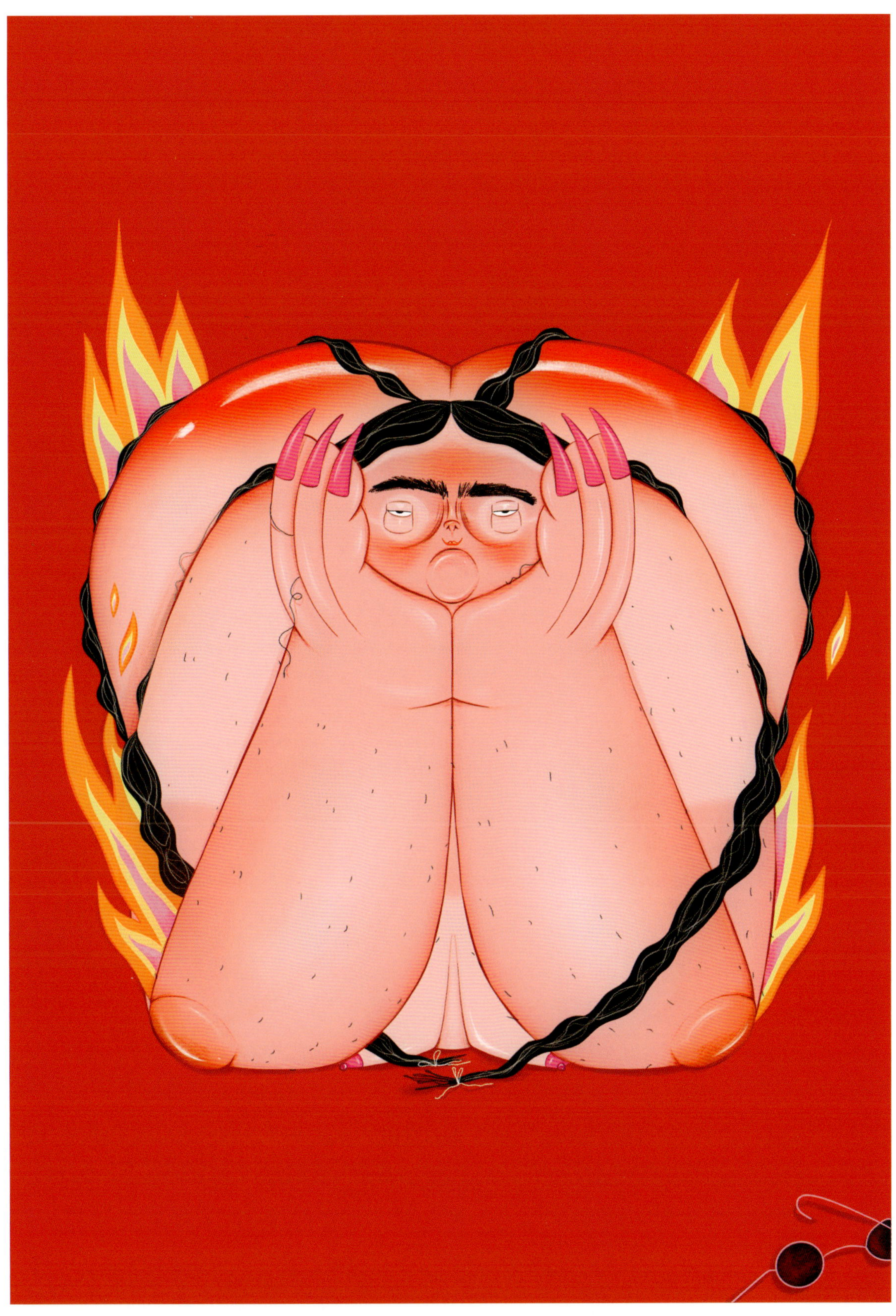

Today Is A Good Day To Burn Down The Patriarchy_(2024_Digital_210 x 297 mm).jpg

Soft_(2022_Digital_210 x 297 mm).jpg

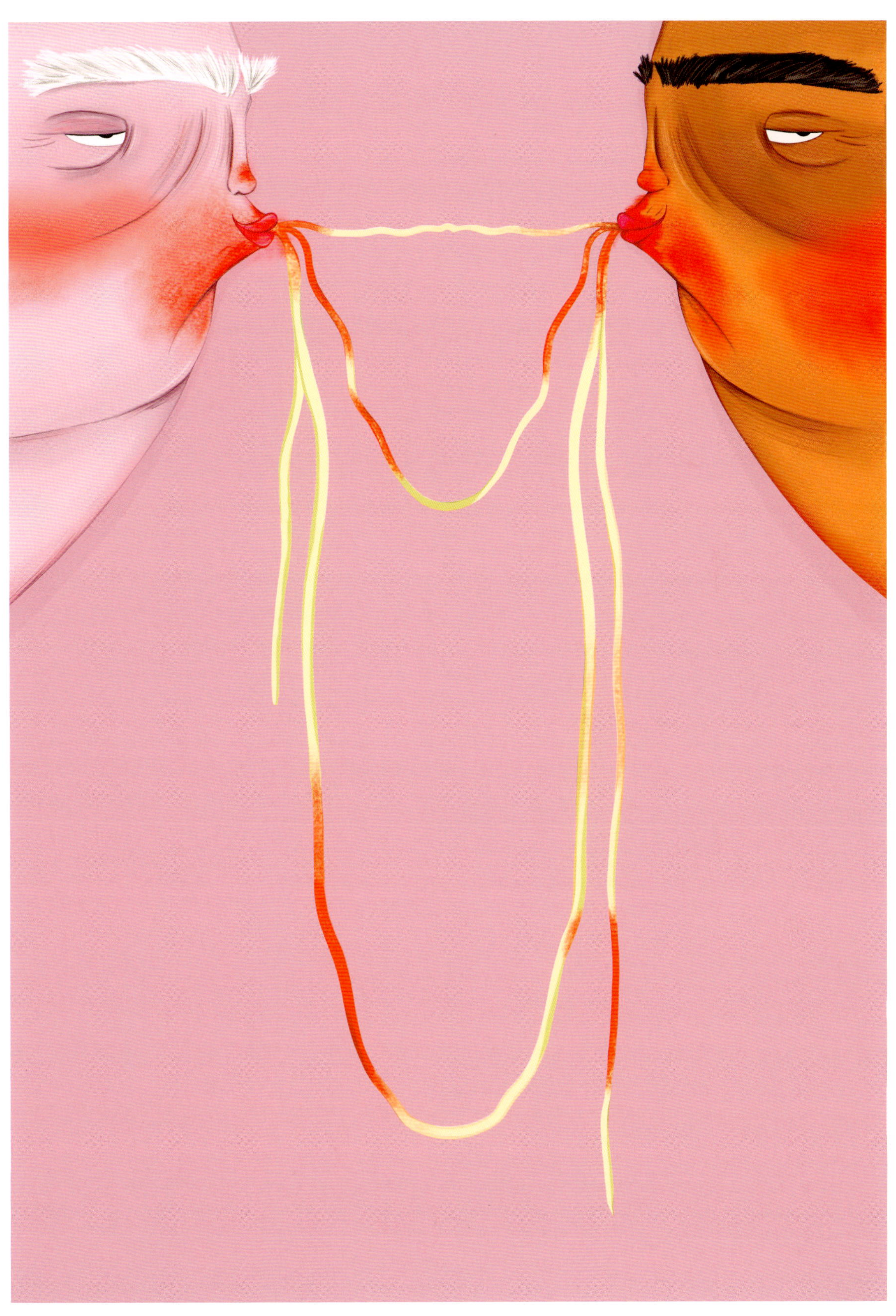

Spaghetti_(2021_Digital_210 x 297 mm).jpg

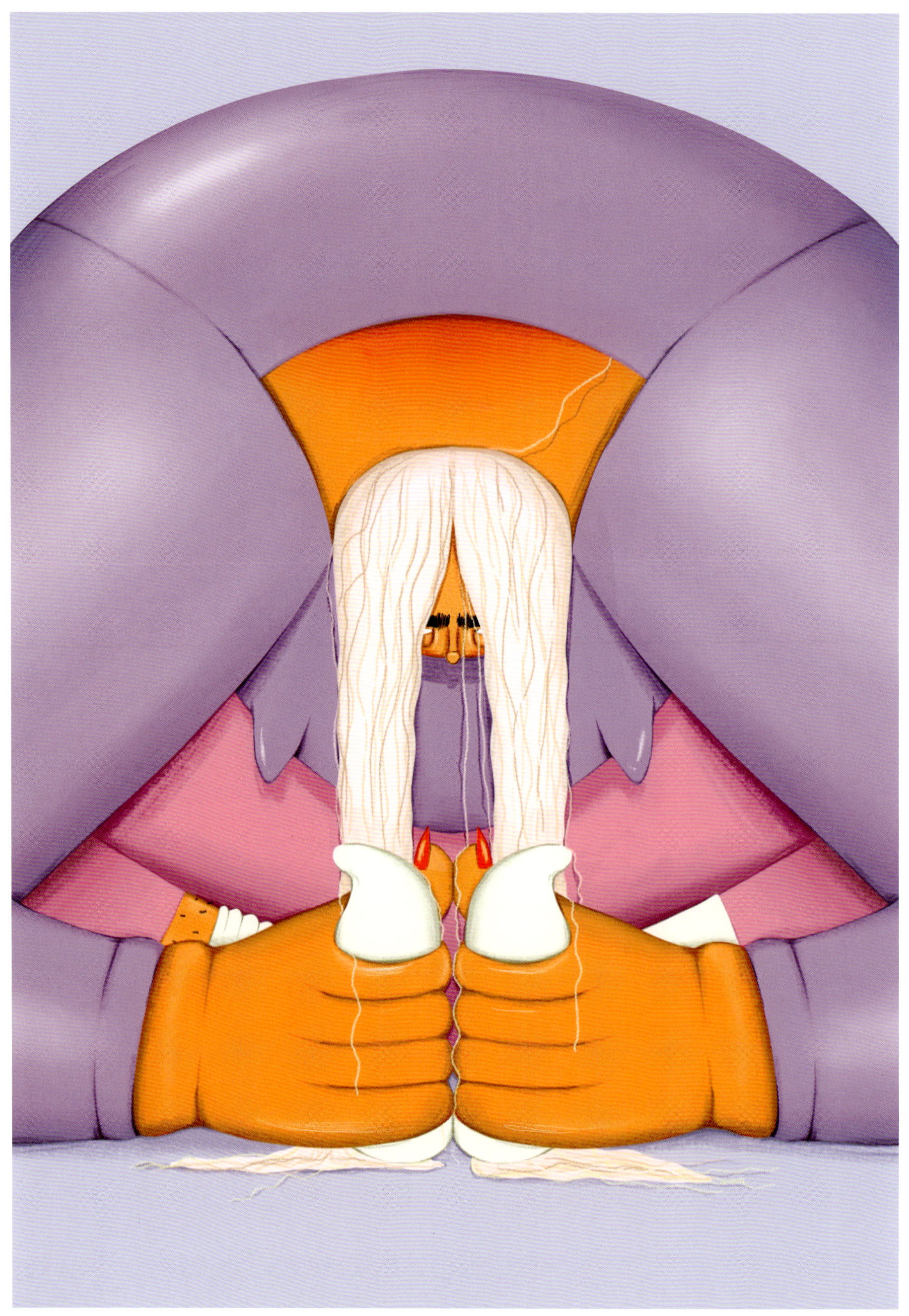



This Pose Is Called "Don't Bother Me"_(2022_Digital_210 x 297 mm).jpg

The Best Part About Gardening Is That You Don't Have To Talk To Anyone_
(2023_Digital_210 x 297 mm).jpg

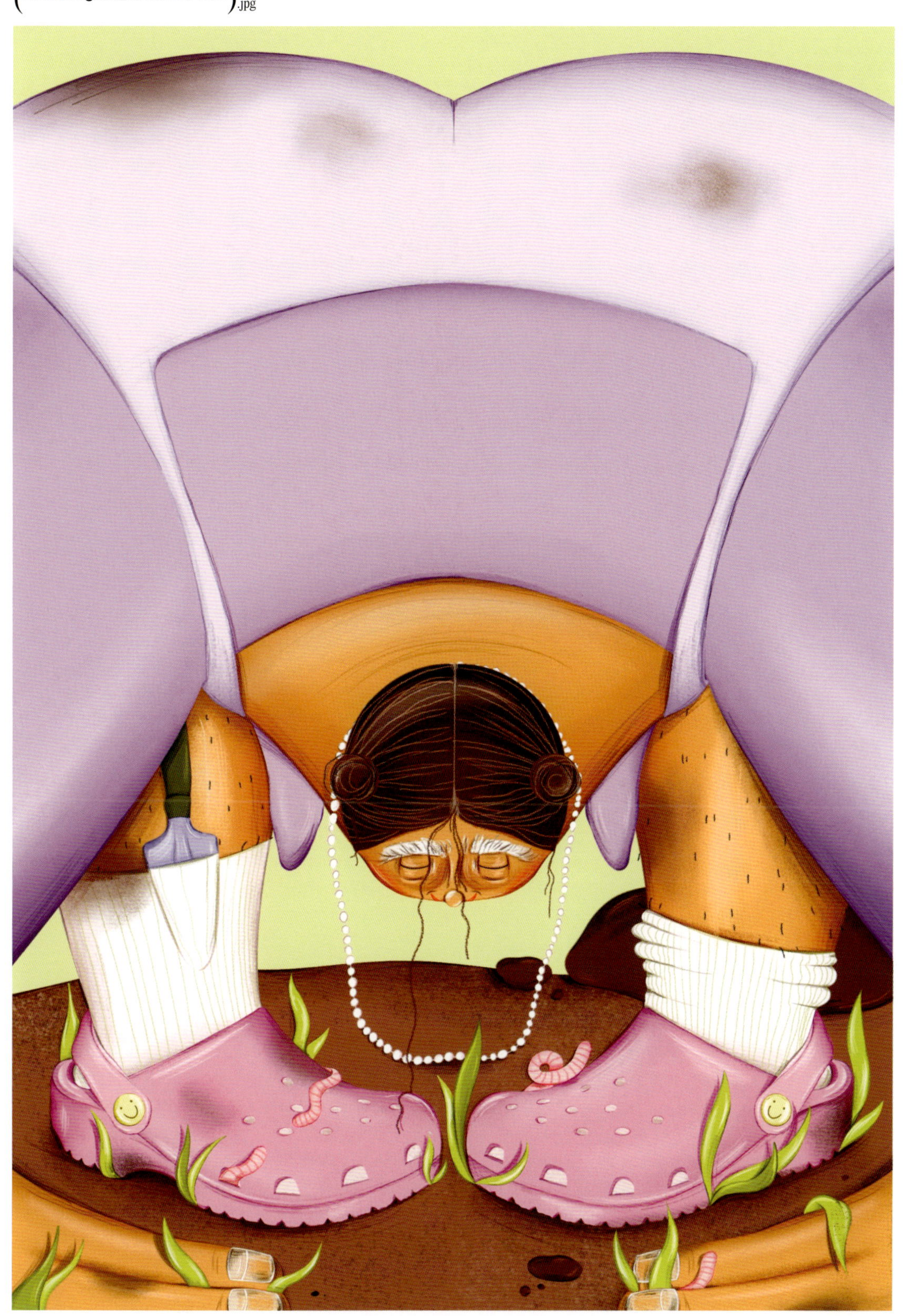

"I don't think too much about whether my work is pretty or ugly, it just comes out looking one way or the other when I put pen to paper."

## Steph Hope

Based in Norway, Steph Hope is an English animator, illustrator, and musician, known for her surreal, hand-drawn style. A Young Guns 17 winner, her short, "Not Drifting Off", was screened at Annecy and Pictoplasma. She co-founded FUS!Animation and is now with Bacon Productions. Working with clients like Channel 4 and FX, she blends analogue techniques with digital polish.

Unknown_(2022_Pen, Paper, Digital_210 x 305 mm).jpg

Cat_(2019_Pen, Paper, Digital_297 x 420 mm).jpg

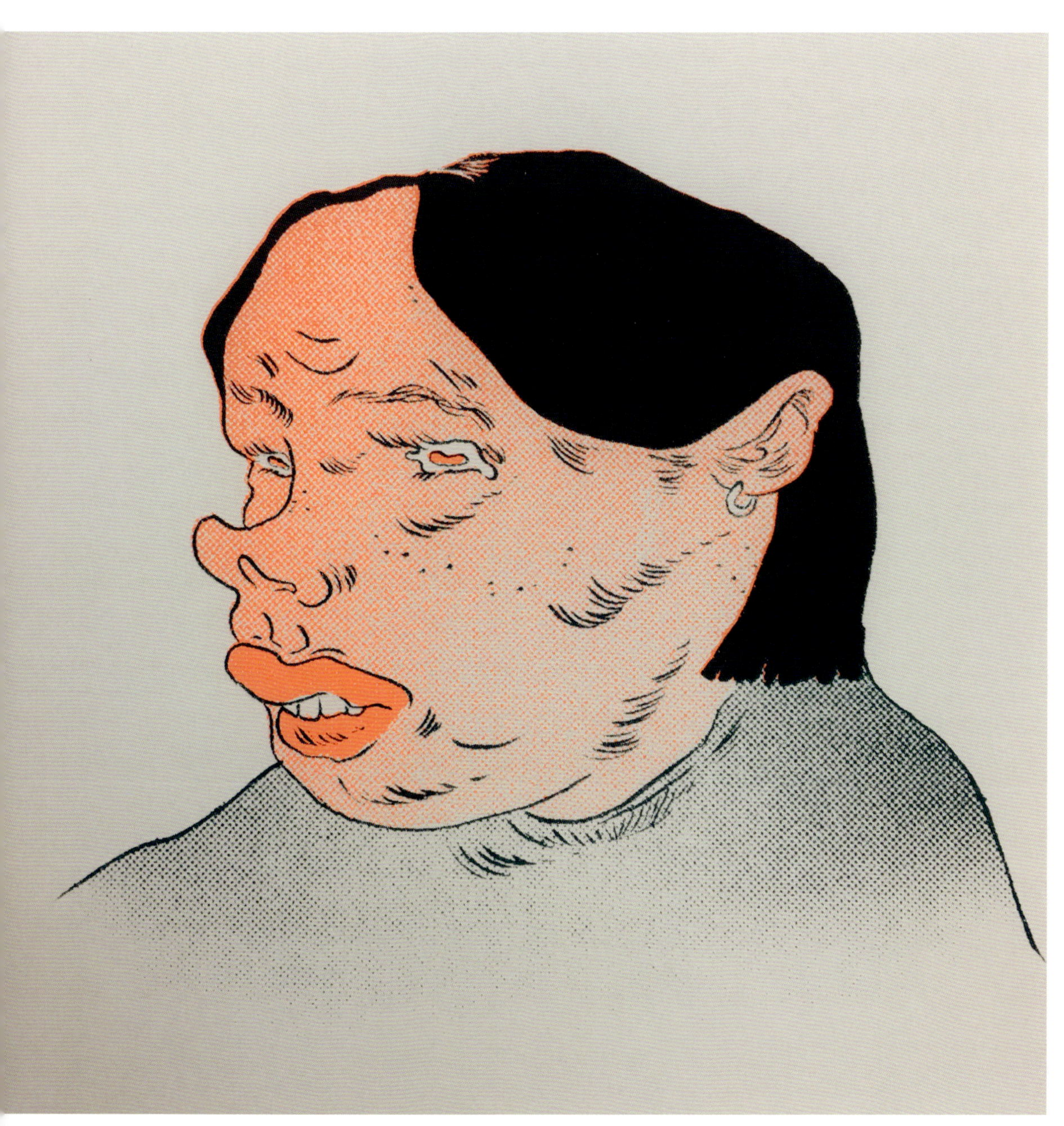

Untitled_(2019_Two-colour Screenprinting_180 x 180 mm).jpg

Untitled_(2015_Pen, Paper, Digital_420 x 593 mm).jpg

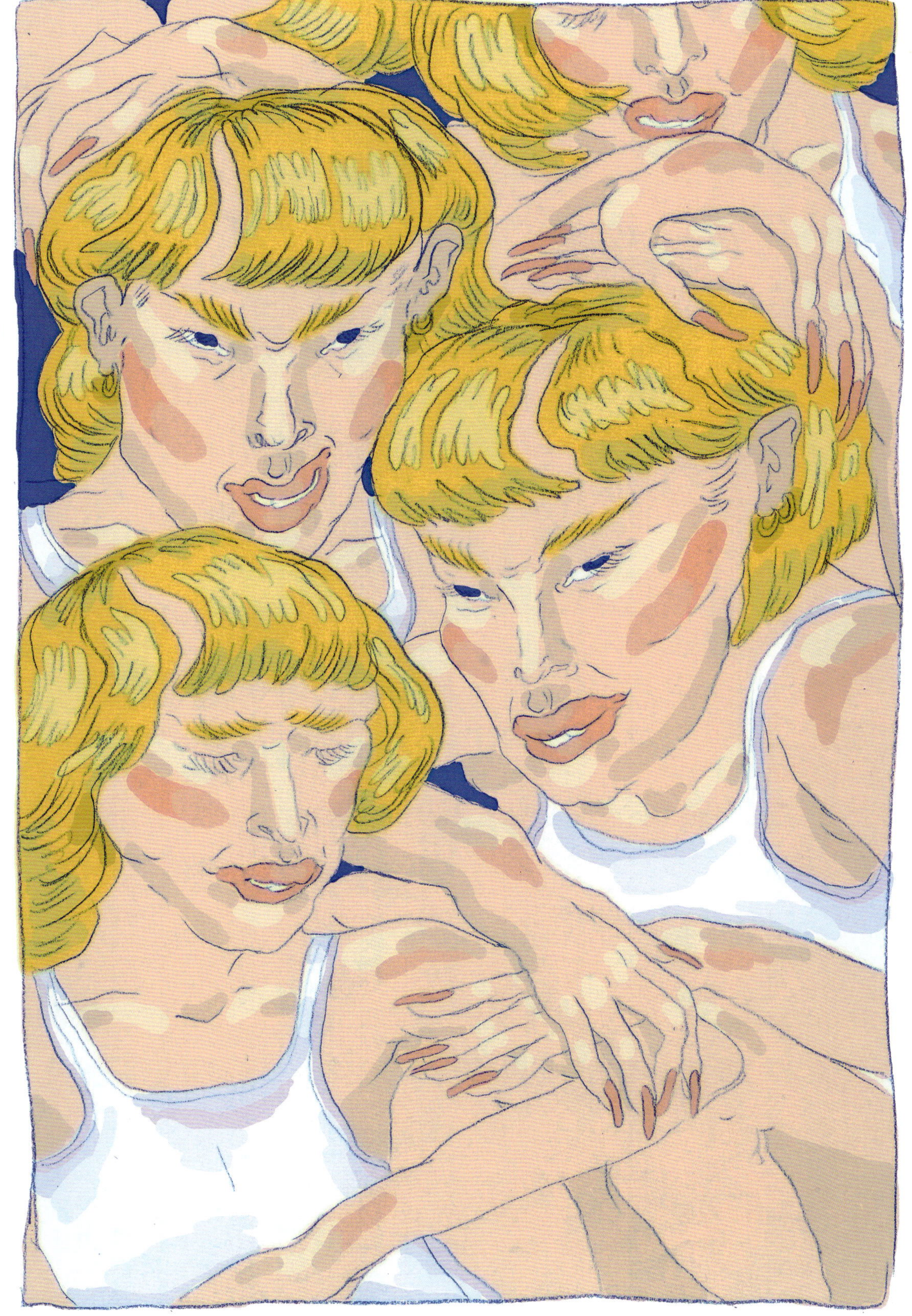

Summer Friends_(2019_Pen, Paper, Digital_210 x 297 mm).jpg

Squished Nisse_(2019_Gouache Paint, Digital_420 x 297 mm).jp

Client: D2 Magasin

"'Pretty ugly' can be extremely grotesque, or a balance between beauty and ugliness. Challenging the fixed norms of beauty expands its definition—and that courage deserves recognition."

LAZY BUG

LAZY BUG, born in Taipei City in 1997, creates vivid, high-contrast works using flat painting, mixed media, and installation. Her use of semi-automatic techniques and material contrasts heightens visual clarity, while bold colours and layered textures define her atmospheric, emotionally charged compositions.

Garden Elf_(2022_Acrylic, Canvas_1620 x 1300 mm).jpg

Die Ski_(2023_Acrylic, Canvas_605 x 500 mm).jpg

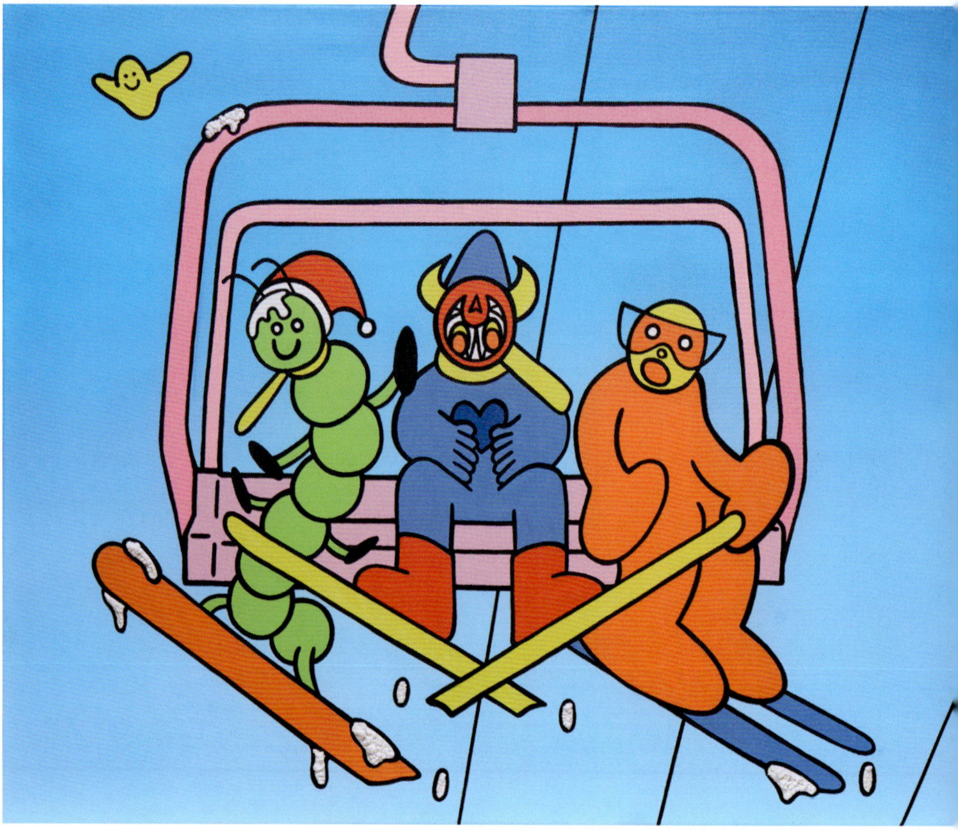

End Of Month_(2023_Acrylic, Canvas_450 x 380 mm).jpg

Fortune Teller_(2022_Acrylic, Canvas_1300 x 970 mm).jpg

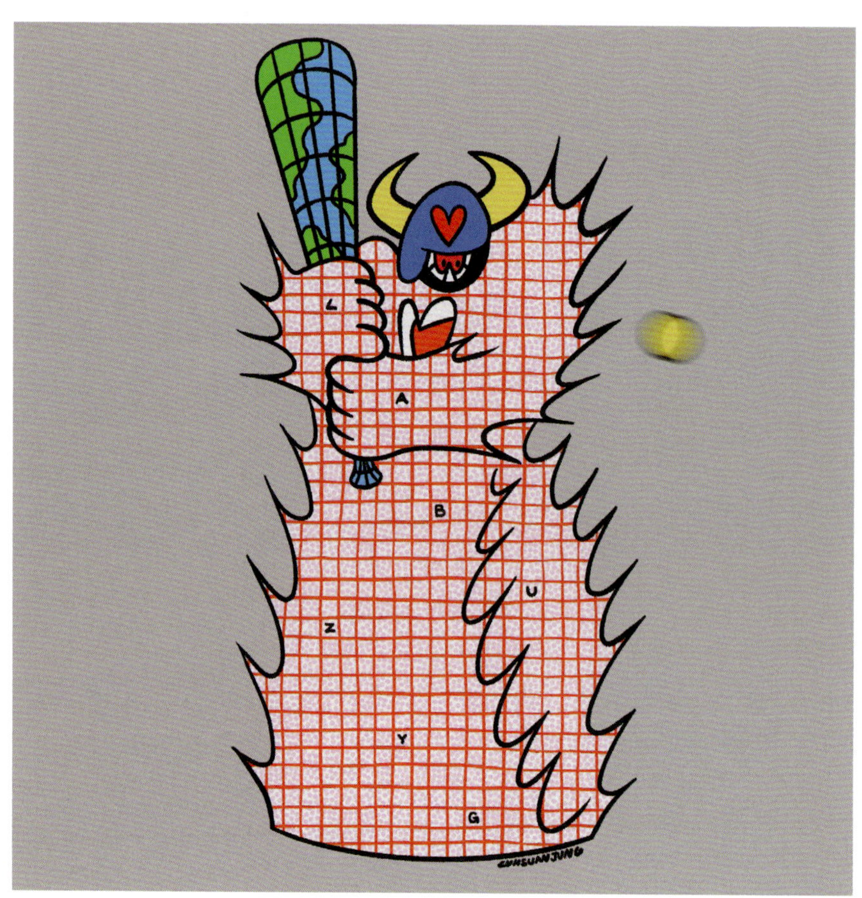


Man Of The World_(2024_Digital_2048 x 2048 px).jpg

Rumble_(2025_Acrylic, Canvas_450 x 380 mm).jpg

Push_(2024_Digital_2480 x 3508 px).jpg

Silent Protest_(2022_Acrylic, Canvas_450 x 380 mm).jp

I'm Fine_(2023_Acrylic, Canvas_450 x 380 mm).jpg

Twins_(2023_Acrylic, Canvas_605 x 500 mm).jpg

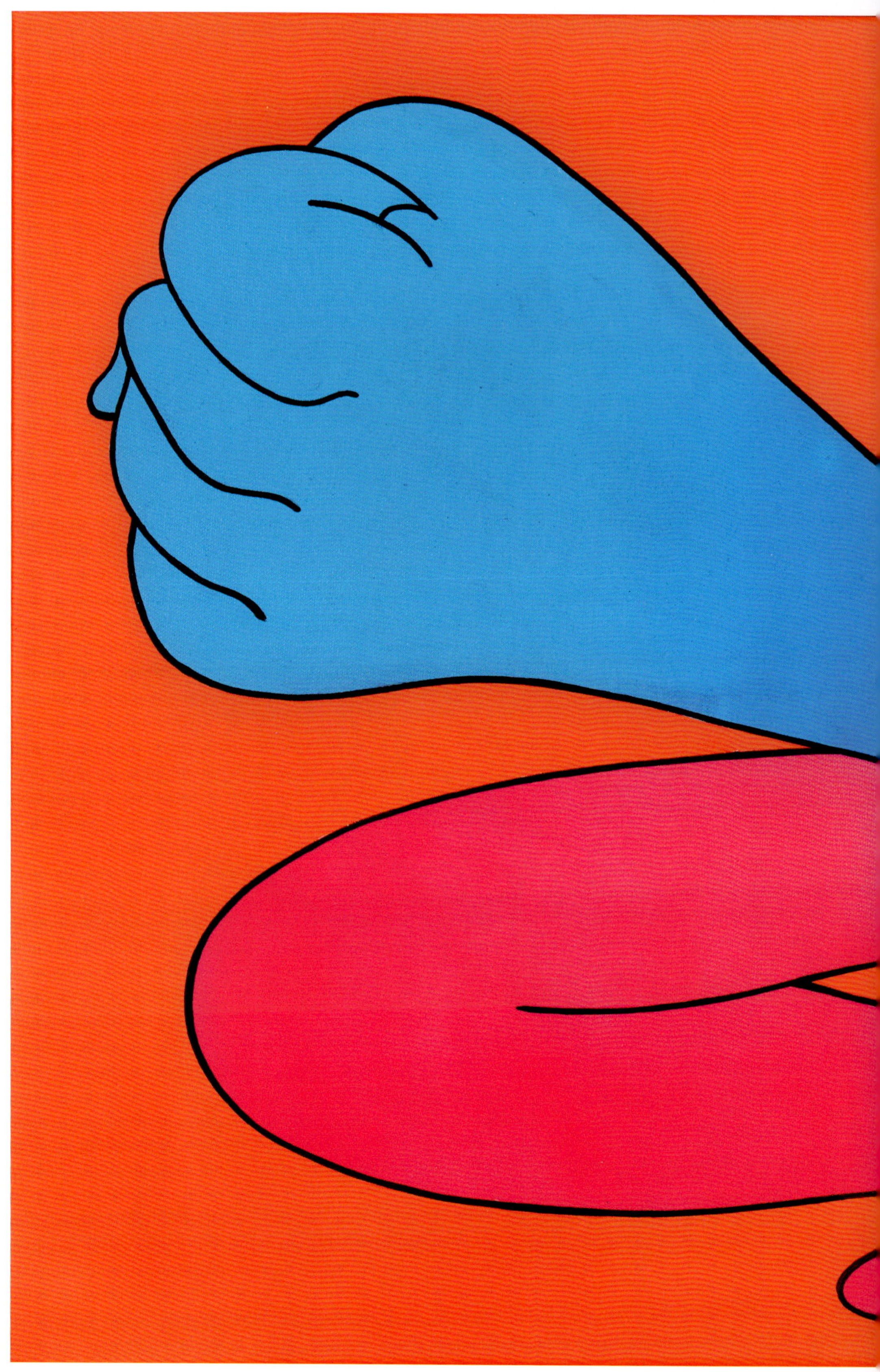

One Big Step_(2024_Acrylic, Canvas_645 x 355 mm).jpg

"'Pretty ugly' is when something's so wrong it loops back around to feeling right again. It's awkward, a bit gross, but full of character."

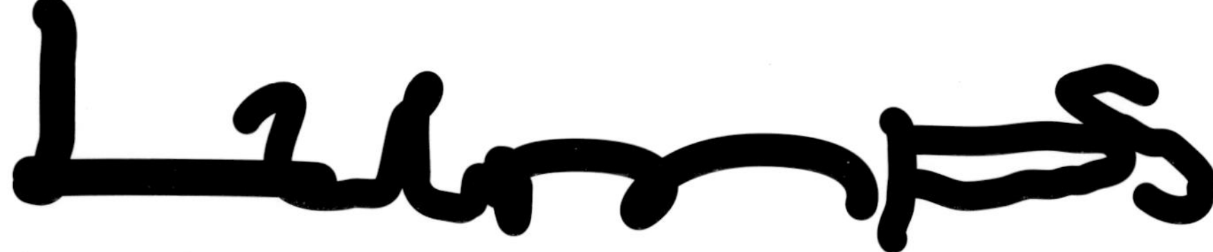

Lumps

Sam Drew, aka Lumps, is a London-based illustrator, animator, and creative director. Fusing surreal visuals with playful design, his work spans illustration, sculpture, and animation. With 10+ years of experience, he has collaborated with clients like The New York Times and Business Insider, while building a distinctive art brand with a dedicated online following.

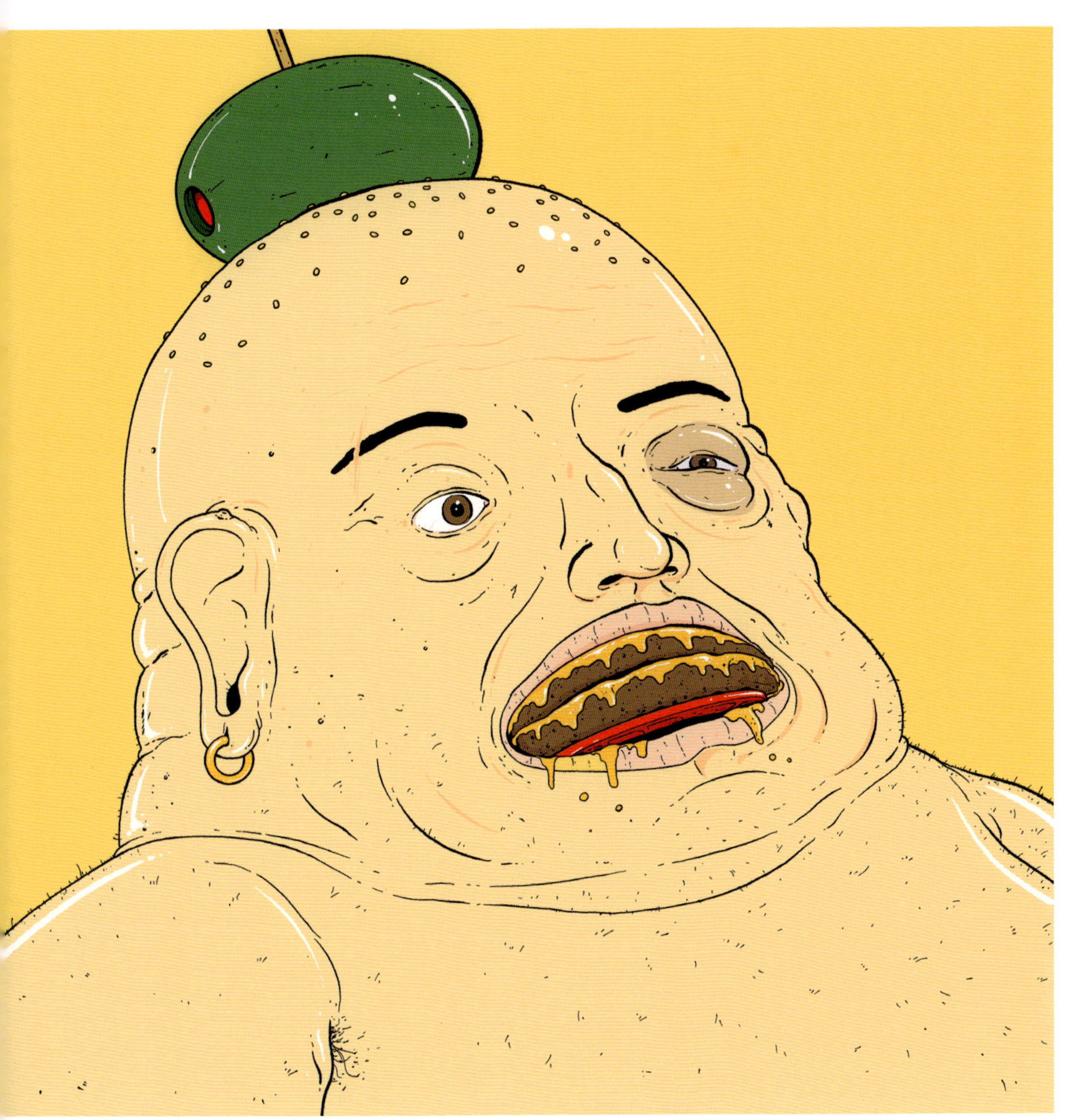

Burger Man_(2023_Digital_3600 x 3600 px).jpg

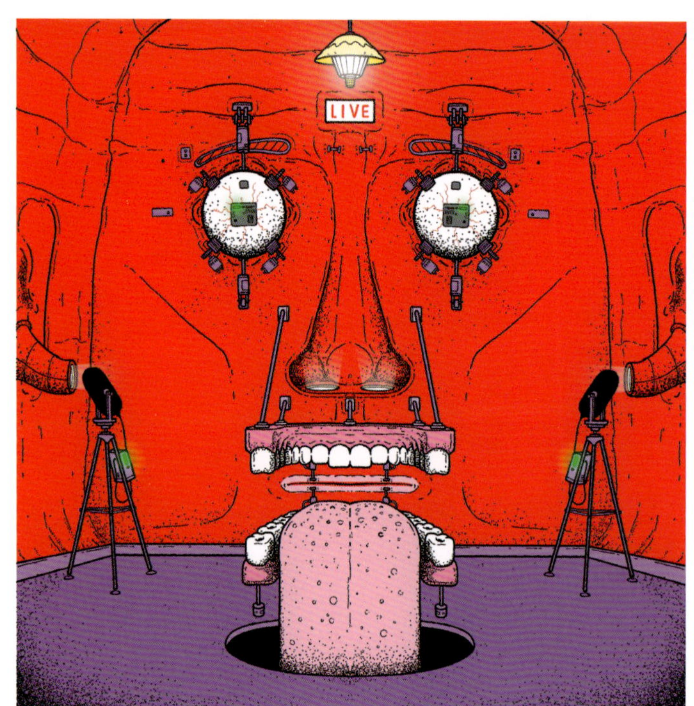


Head Interior_(2022_Digital_2000 x 2000 px).jpg

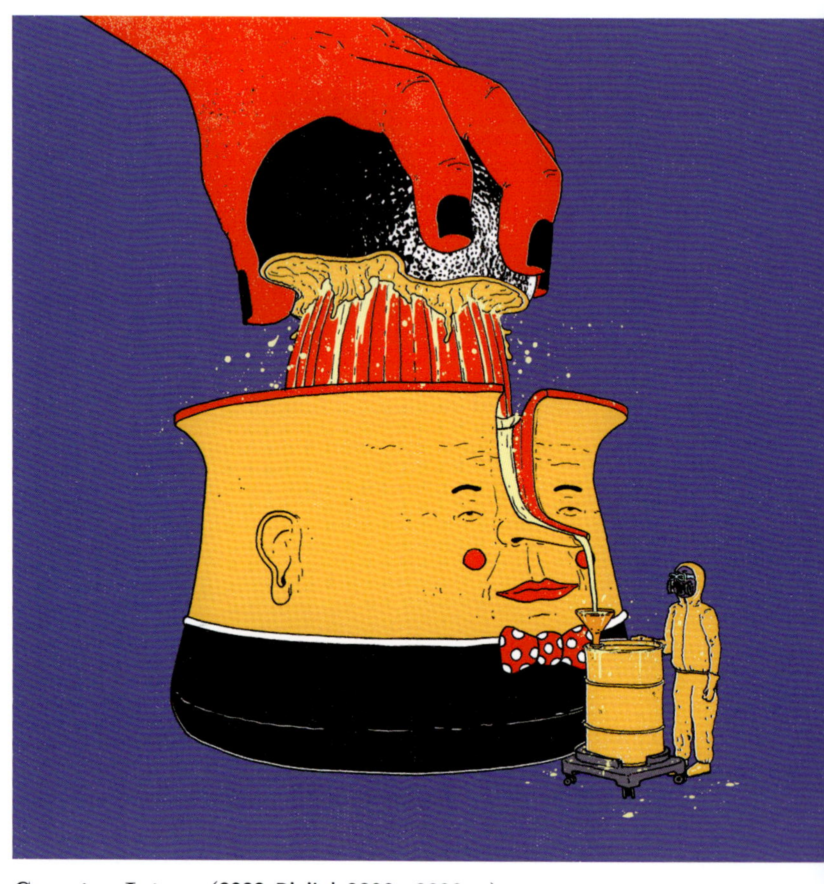

Creative Juice_(2023_Digital_3600 x 3600 px).jpg

Lump Land_(2023_Digital_3600 x 3600 px).jpg

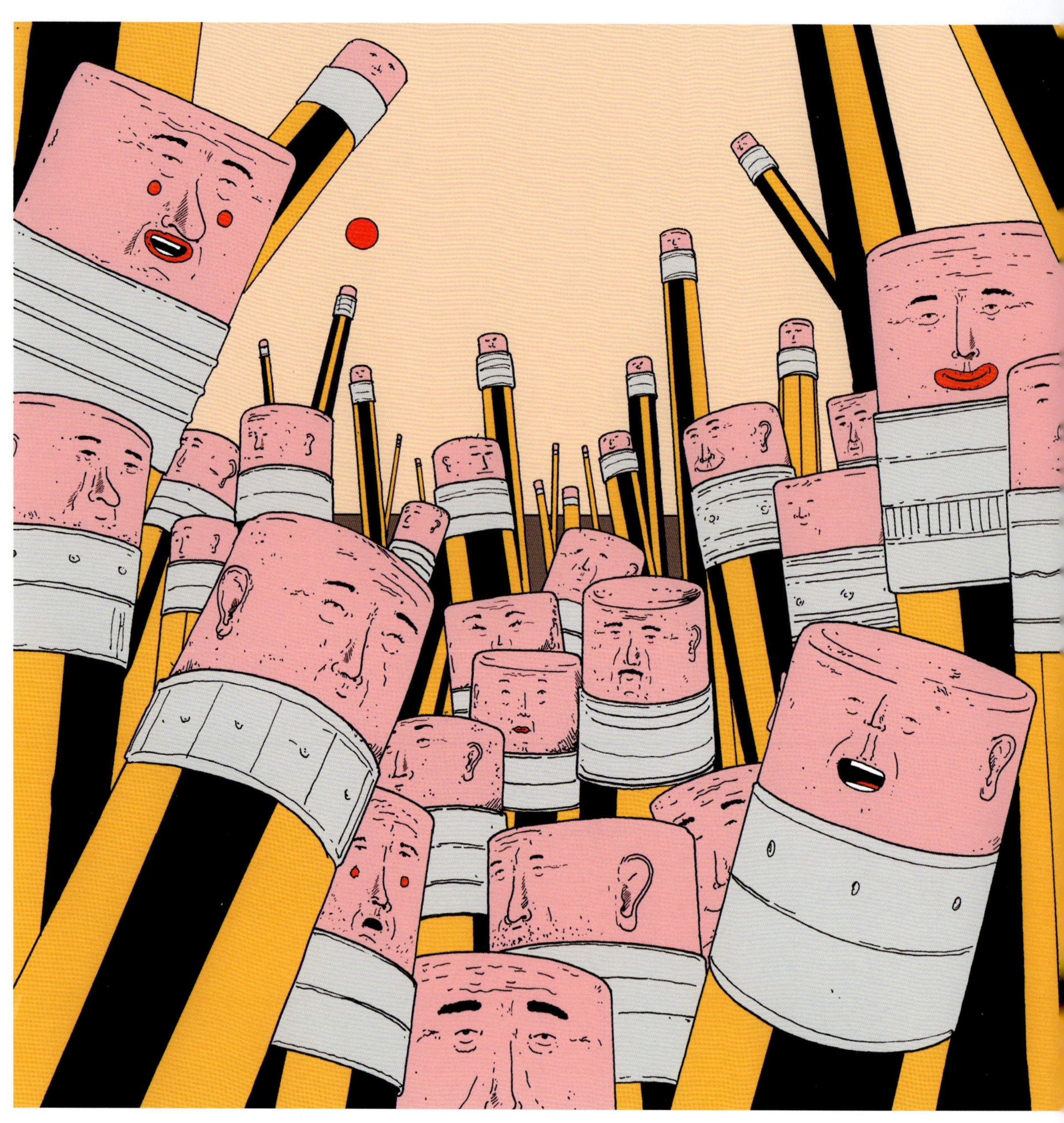

Pencil Pot_(2023_Digital_3600 x 3600 px).jpg

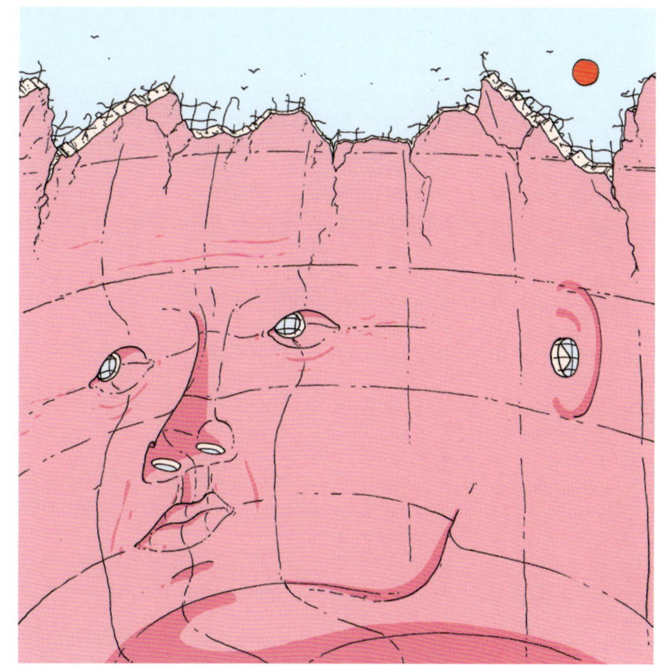

Inside Head_(2020_Digital_3600 x 3600 px).jpg

Trying to Sleep_(2020_Digital_2943 x 2896 px).jpg

Lumpy Tea Party_(2019_Digital_9933 x 7016 px).jp

BANG

“[‘Pretty ugly’] feels like the creator’s passion and intent came through—so I’d take that as a compliment.”

Shinkichi Hiroshima

Hiroshima Shinkichi is a Saitama-based artist using acrylic and airbrush to depict surreal moments from daily life—where bright colours and playful patterns contrast with ambiguous, often darker emotions. His characters appear caught in "re-alistic fiction"—unfolding scenes that feel both familiar and strange. His work has been exhibited internationally, with solo shows in London, Tokyo, and Norwich.

)ccupied_(2023_Acrylic, Canvas_2000 × 2000 mm).jpg

The Stripper_(2023_Acrylic, Canvas_1455 × 1455 mm).jp

Uninvited_(2023_Acrylic, Canvas_1167 × 910 mm).jpg

Spacing Out_(2022_Acrylic, Canvas_910 × 727 mm)

Errorist_(2022_Acrylic, Canvas_910 × 1167 mm).jpg

Keep Your Eyes On The Road_(2023_Acrylic, Canvas_1600 × 1300 mm).jpg

Fall Out Of Love_(2024_Acrylic, Canvas_1800 x 1800 mm).jpg

Bread Thief_(2023_Acrylic, Canvas_1940 x 1120 mm).jpg

"'Pretty ugly' is the sweet spot where charm meets chaos. It's about finding beauty in flaws, character in imperfections—where things aren't perfect, but they're full of personality."

Gaetan Sahsah

Gaetan Sahsah is a freelance illustrator based in Albi, France. His work blends clean lines, playful colours, and bold storytelling, often balancing innocence with provocation. He collaborates with international clients across editorial, branding, and personal projects.

Cool Dog_(2024_Digital_2478 x 3508 px).jpg

Don't Think Too Much_(2023_Digital_3508 x 3508 px).jp

Attic Stories — Album Cover_(2023_Digital_3508 x 3508 px).jpg

088

New World_(2025_Digital_2479 x 3508 px).jpg

Noble Heart_(2024_Digital_2506 x 3508 px).jpg

090 Håkan Hellström — Live Poster_(2023_Digital_2478 x 3508 px).jpg

Magic Bus — Escape Game Poster_(2023_Digital_2368 x 3508 px).jpg

"Some things can be revolting, yet you find yourself unable to look away—giving you just enough time to notice the beauty hidden in the details."

YONK

YONK is a 3D animation studio known for its playful, maximalist style shaped by Virtual Reality Sculpting. Their work merges raw, childlike forms with polished, vibrant finishes. By breaking from traditional 3D norms, they create striking characters and animations that are bold, unconventional, and delightfully strange.

Date_(2022_Digital_3480 x 3508 px).jpg

Portrait One_(2022_Digital_3480 x 3508 px).jpg

Portrait Two_(2022_Digital_3480 x 3508 px).jpg

Sunflowers_(2023_Digital_3480 x 3508 px).jpg

Nature Guy_(2023_Digital_3480 x 3508 px).jpg

Spotlight
special feature

@gregory_jacobsen ✺ Gregory Jacobsen is a Chicago-based painter known for grotesque, hyper-detailed works that explore bodily excess and theatricality. His art has been shown internationally, including at the Long Beach Museum of Art and Casino Luxembourg. He has created album covers for experimental musicians and is featured in collections like MoMA and the Antoine de Galbert Foundation.

Q & A

Could you share a little bit about your background/journey so far with our readers? How has your creative expression evolved over the years until you arrived at your current aesthetic/artistic style and medium(s) you work with?

I've always had some sort of creative pursuit going on when I was a kid—drawing was the most accessible. I've long been fascinated in the weird, grotesque, and humorous aspects of art, from MAD Magazine to a film like Bad Taste.

My aesthetic has remained consistent since I was young; I've just refined it over the years. I love the crass and vulgar, but I also appreciate beauty and form. "Beauty"—in this context—refers to something that is aesthetically pleasing—something you can't look away from, that touches you on a deeper, more primitive level, whether it be conventional, experimental, or crude and ugly.

I dabble in other mediums, but painting is my main focus. It allows me to get messy, get experimental, to erase and build back up. My mode of thinking and working is non-linear. The paint is essential for pulling an image out of nothing. The image evolves out of the process.

A

Why do you think society is increasingly drawn to unconventional aesthetics and what does it say about our culture?

I wish this was true. Or at least it's difficult to make such a blanket assessment. It all goes in waves and maybe we're on a more homogenous wave right now? In the United States at least, ugh. There will always be small pockets of people that seek out the unconventional—I don't know. Interest in my work comes and goes. I do love that I have a good amount of crossover appeal, where my work really speaks to someone that I would least expect to be interested in what I'm doing.

How would you personally define the term "pretty ugly"?

"Pretty ugly" is finding attraction in repulsion. It's about a primal emotional response to what is outside the norms of what society considers "beautiful."

How do you see the "pretty ugly" aesthetic evolving in the future, and what impact could it have on our world on a broader scale?

When I was an art student, I wrote endless essays about how the grotesque and unconventional was a path to utopia where people would express themselves more truthfully. It was going to change the world! I thought anything that was harmonious or pretty was false and empty. But as I met more people and gained more life experience, I realised not everyone thinks the way I do—and that I wasn't unearthing some universal truth. I was being reactive, trying to give intellectual weight to the impulses behind my work.

Honestly, I don't know how it will evolve. For me, I am always working towards a visual language that seeps into the mainstream. I used to think this was a bad thing and that these sorts of aesthetics should be closed off to anyone not willing to immerse themselves into the subculture because it ultimately becomes dumbed down and grossly commodified, making the gestures irrelevant and empty.

I now believe it's important for these aesthetics to infiltrate the mainstream, to be accepted and to be the norm. I have lived my life for so long intentionally on the outside, simply because that was the only way I knew how to survive. I had to be in my safe little pocket. What is progress if you're going to gatekeep it? I guess I'm still wanting that utopia I was writing about thirty years ago.

A

What advice would you give to emerging artists who want to break away from conventional beauty standards in their work? How can they stay truly authentic when surrounded by noise?

I think an artist has to have a genuine love for the unconventional. I think that will shine in their work in a very authentic way. What I put into my work is what I see as normal. It's how my brain works, and it's important to tap into that. I also incorporate elements that obsess me to an almost fetishistic level. You need to be obsessed. Your obsession can be something totally mundane and ordinary, but once you put your full personality into it, the funny little idiosyncratic elements will bubble to the surface.

A

Fancy Gelato Gang_(2021_Oil, Panel_914.4 x 609.6 mm).tif

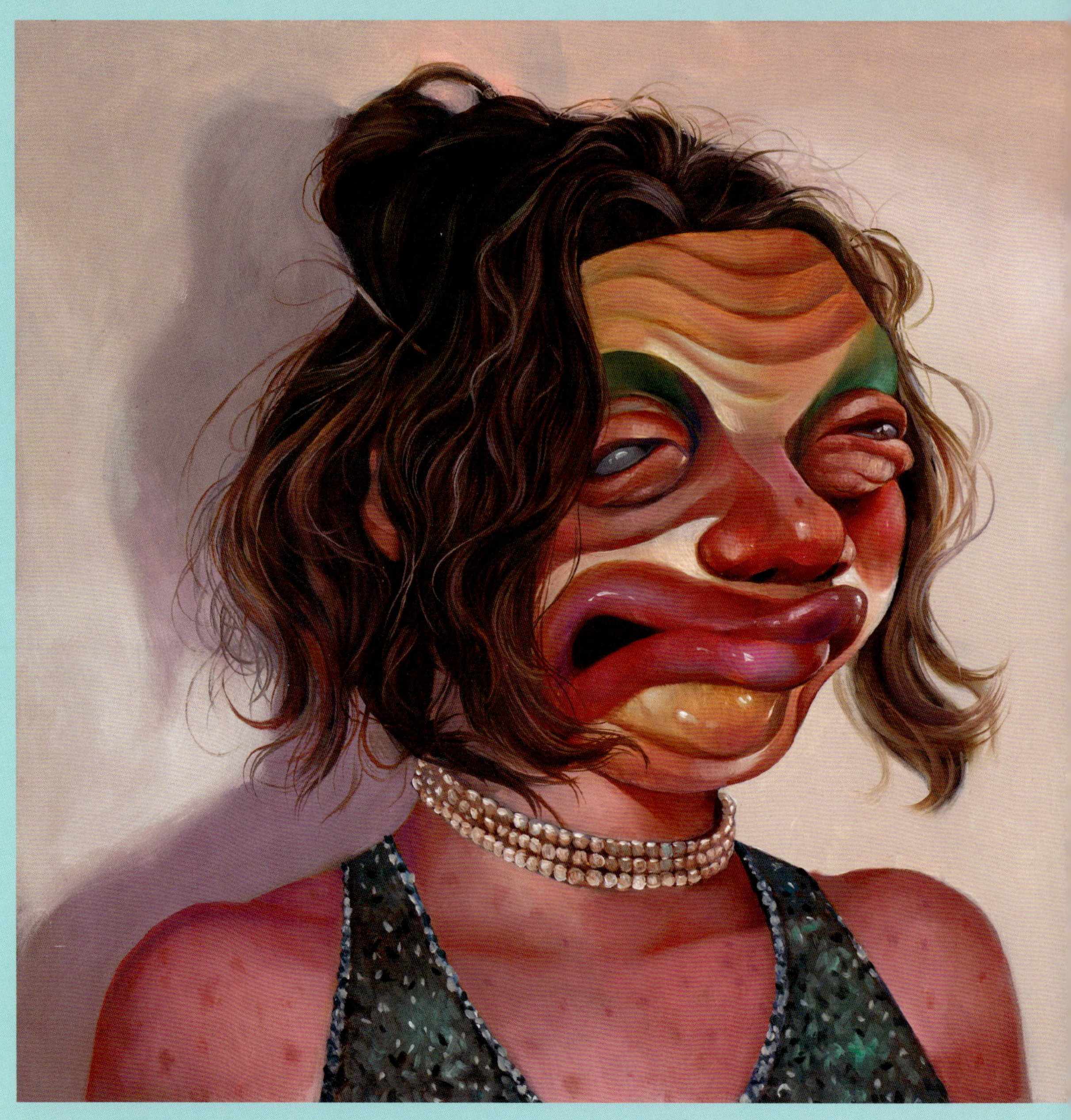

Fancy Night_(2020_Oil, Panel_304.8 x 304.8 mm).tif

Ms Chlorine_(2017_Oil, Panel_152.4 x 152.4 mm).tif

Double Squash Face_(2016_Oil, Panel_152.4 x 152.4 mm).tif

Bedazzled Head_(2020_Oil, Canvas_254 x 254 mm).tif

VICTORY

The Summer Wind Came Blowing In_(2017_Oil, Canvas_1219.2 x 1828.8 mm).tif

Pinky_(2023_Oil, Panel_152.4 x 152.4 mm).tif

Duckie_(2022_Oil, Panel_152.4 x 152.4 mm).tif

Lilli_(2018_Oil, Panel_152.4 x 152.4 mm).tif

Gurney_(2022_Oil, Panel_152.4 x 152.4 mm).tif

Princess Sissi Overalls_(2023_Oil, Panel_152.4 x 152.4 mm).tif

Beautiful Hair_(2021_Oil, Linen_406.4 x 304.8 mm).tif

Garbage Face_(2024_Oil, Panel_457.2 x 457.2 mm).tif

Gaggle_(2017_Oil, Panel_547.2 x 609.6 mm).tif

"For me, 'pretty ugly' is not a negative or derogatory term. I define it as a hidden gem—an element that allows one to express their unique personality, humour, and way of thinking."

BON

BON is a self-taught illustrator based in Tokyo, working freelance since graduating university. Her playful, distinctive style features across a wide range of projects—from craft beer labels and izakaya glassware to corporate illustrations. Beyond commissions, she also creates and sells illustrated merchandise like T-shirts and stickers, blending commercial and personal work with a unique touch.

Band-aid_(2024_Digital_254 × 254 mm).jpg

Pea Sprout_(2024_Digital_254 × 254 mm).jpg

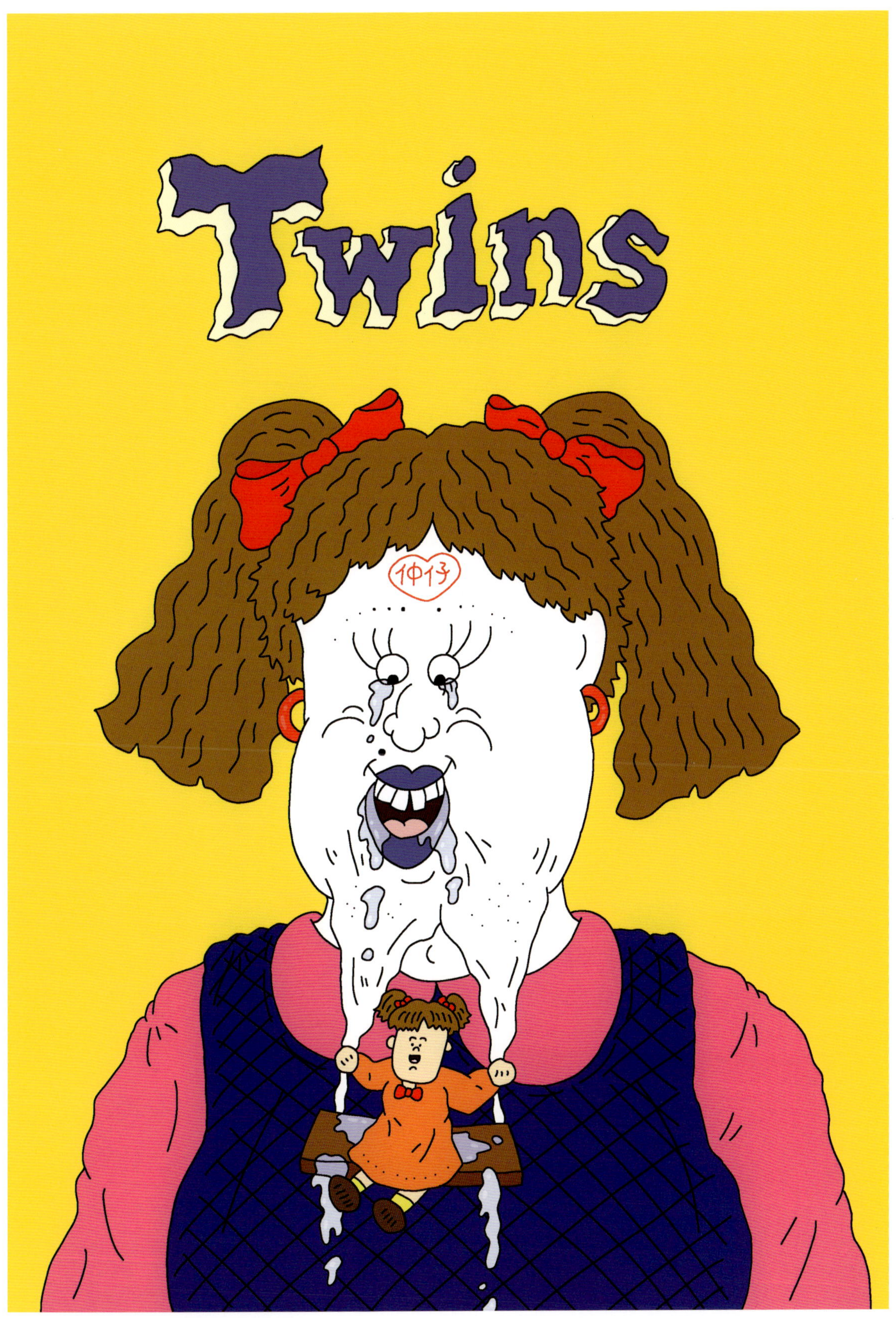


Twins_(2022_Digital_185 × 264 mm).jpg

Puzzle_(2024_Digital_185 × 278 mm).jpg

Tetris Game_(2024_Digital_254 × 254 mm).jpg

Becon And Eggs_(2024_Digital_254 × 254 mm).jp

Neapolitan_(2022_Digital_254 × 254 mm).jpg

"In my work, 'pretty' and 'ugly' are two sides of the same coin. I often address dark or unsettling themes, but always with a sense of humour and a vibrant colour palette. A spoonful of sugar helps the medicine go down."

## Dan Lydersen

Dan Lydersen is an American painter based in Sacramento, California. He studied at the American University of Rome and holds degrees from UC Santa Cruz and the San Francisco Art Institute. His work has been exhibited widely, including solo shows at Jack Fischer Gallery in San Francisco and Thinkspace Projects in Los Angeles.

Hanalei Hoodoo_(2023_Oil, Wood Panel_610 x 610 mm).jpg

Solana Slurm_(2022_Oil, Wood Panel_355 x 355 mm).jpg

)rkney Amble_(2022_Oil, Wood Panel_355 x 355 mm).jpg

Spree de Corpse_(2023_Oil, Wood Panel_355 x 279 mm).j

Inglorious Rex_(2023_Oil, Wood Panel_355 x 279 mm).jpg

Klabauterkatze_(2023_Oil, Wood Panel_305 x 305 mm).jpg

Fizzlebloom Luau_(… Oil, Wood Panel_610 x … ).jpg

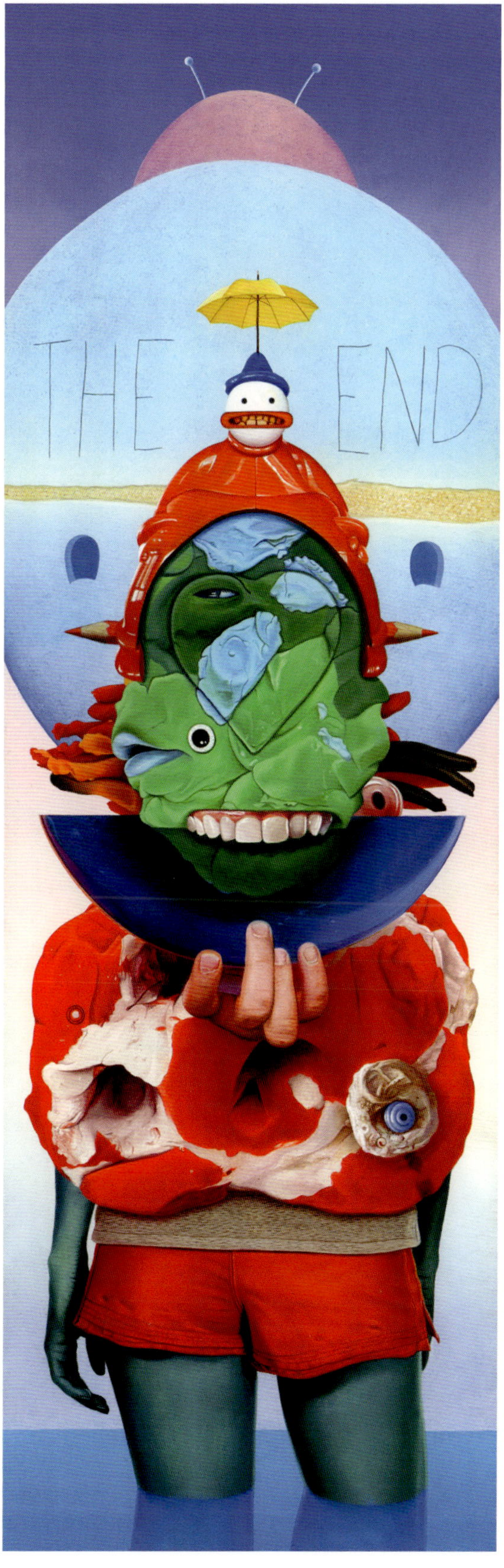

Exit Reprobus_(2023_Oil, Wood Panel_610 x 203 mm).jpg

“Nothing is ugly; it’s all a matter of how the person sees things around them.”

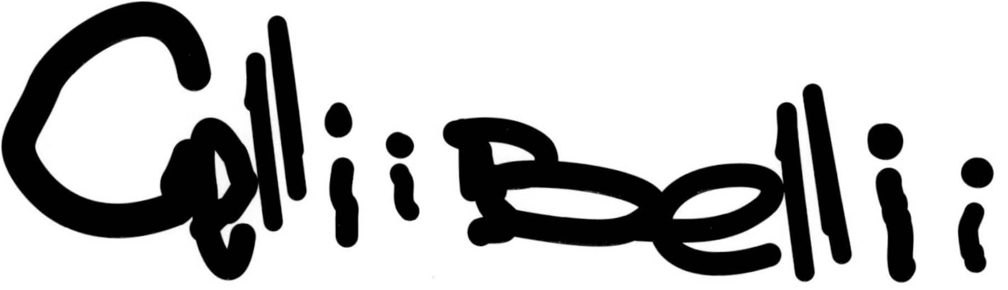


Cellii Belli

Celine is an illustrator and designer based in Cairo. Inspired by storytelling and emotion, she mixes different media to creat her signature style. Her work includes posters, album covers, and character designs. Her posters were selected in the 10 Best Arabic Posters Competition (Rounds 3 & 4), and she was featured by It’s Nice That in 2021.

Spicy Noodles Challenge_(2021_Ink, Digital_2580 x 3508 px).jpg

"Cocoon" In The Process Of Becoming A Beautiful Butterfly_(2021_Ink, Digital_2580 x 3508 px).jpg

Escape_(2021_Ink, Digital_2580 x 3508 px).jpg

New Me_(2021_Ink, Digital_2580 x 3508 px).jpg

Serenity_(2021_Ink, Digital_3508 x 3508 px).jpg

Makhtout_(2021_Ink, Digital_2580 x 3508 px).jpg

Client & Workshop Organiser: Sherine Salla

Pearl Queen_(2022_Ink, Digital_2580 x 3508 px).jpg

"'Pretty ugly' is irony incarnate, a collision of beauty and repulsion that mocks the very idea of aesthetic purity, forcing an encounter with discomfort disguised as allure."

Anu Jakobson

Anu Jakobson's work explores how digital culture and internet aesthetics influence human consciousness. Using airbrushing, she creates soft, fragmented visuals that reflect the unexpected, unfinished feel of the early internet. In contrast to today's sleek digital precision, she embraces the rawness of low-resolution, out-of-context imagery—mirroring the fragmented way the internet shapes memory and perception.

K-hole_(2025_Acrylic, Canvas_600 x 900 mm).jpg Photo: Kaisa Maasik

Applying To Universities Releases Dopamine Into My Bloodstream_
(2024_Acrylics, Canvas_800 x 1000 mm).jpg

Photo: Kaisa Maasik

Untitled_(2025_Acrylic, Canvas_500 x 1000 mm).jpg

Photo: Kaisa Maasik

Petty Bourgeoisie_(2025_ Acrylic, Canvas_700 x 1000 mm).jpg

Photo: Kaisa Maasik

You’re A Dream, Who Was Born Into A Worlds, That Is Also A Dream_(2024_Acrylic, Canvas_600 x 800 mm).jpg

Photo: Kaisa Maasik

A Body Without Organs_(2024_Acrylic, Canvas_500 x 1000 mm).jpg

Untitled_(2025_Acrylic, Canvas_800 x 1000 mm).jpg

Photo: Kaisa Maasik

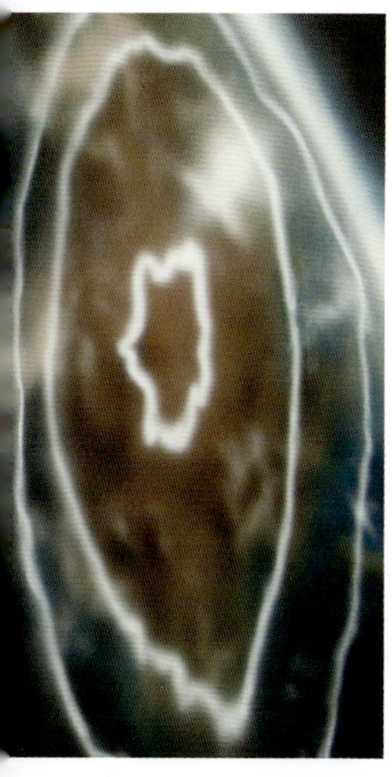

Photo: Kaisa Maasik

"My series of illustrations challenges the usual idea of what's ugly; it shines a different light on the aging body, treating it not as something to fix, but as something natural and worth embracing. For me, 'pretty ugly' means: imperfect in a way that feels real, touching, and honest."

Rachel Sender

Rachel Sender is an editorial illustrator based in Rotterdam, originally from Barcelona. She explores human behaviou through warm, humorous visuals. Her practice spans editorial work and community-building, alongside teaching at Willem de Kooning Academy. Her clients include L.A. Times, TED Talks, El País, de Volkskrant, and Refinery29.

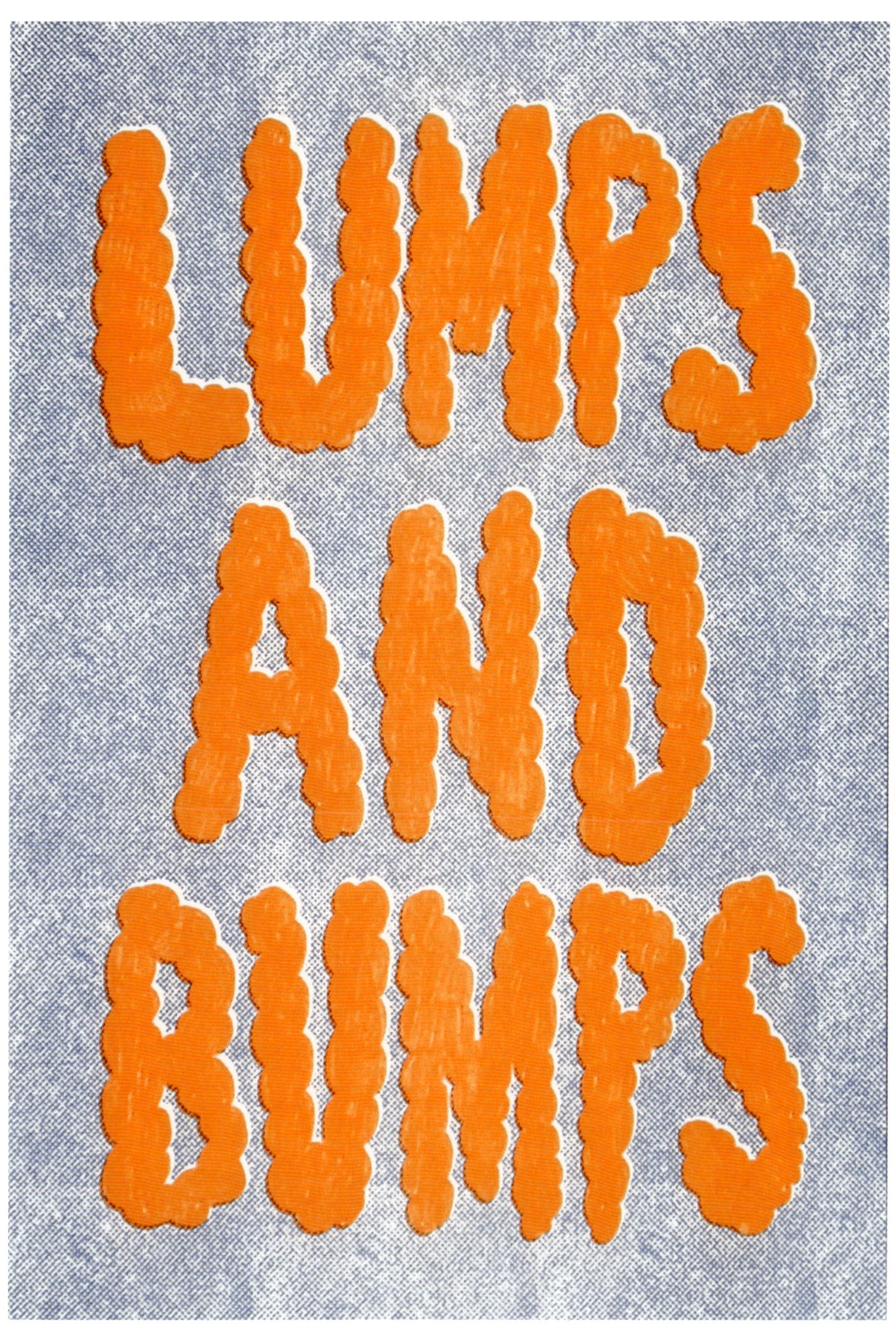


Lumps and Bumps_(2023_Digital, Risograph Printing, Screenprinting_245 x 352 mm).jpg

Risography: Teuntje Floor
Back Card Screenprinting: Michael van Kekem

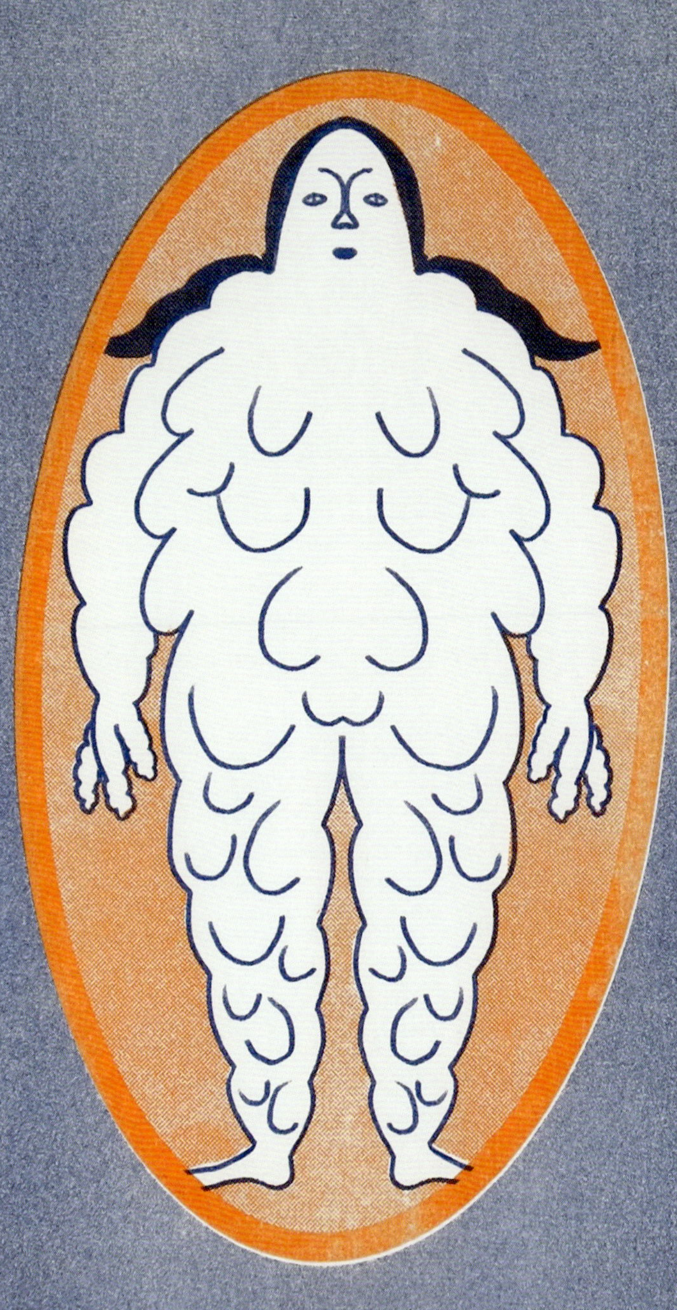

I wake up to find this person
in the mirror. My body is
unfamiliar. It happened quite
suddenly, it's taken new form.

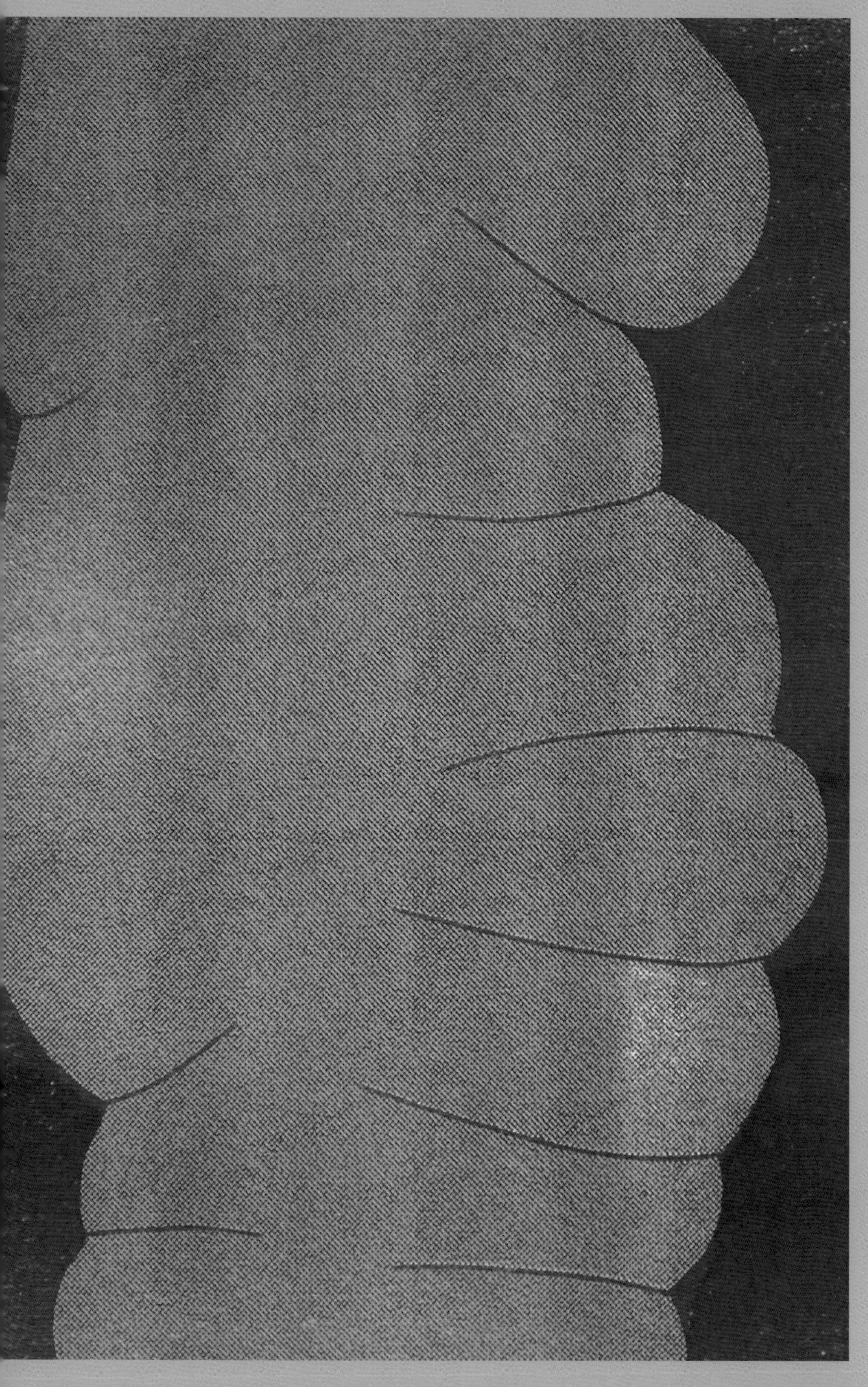

New moles, new rolls, fields of hair. Callous toes tell stories of journeys.

Thinning strands, white and
grey. Age's touch is not gentle;
its grip isn't soft.

Beneath my eyes, luggage bags of sleepless nights. Skin sags, wrinkles expand. Joy and worries etched upon my face, a canvas of years of emotions.

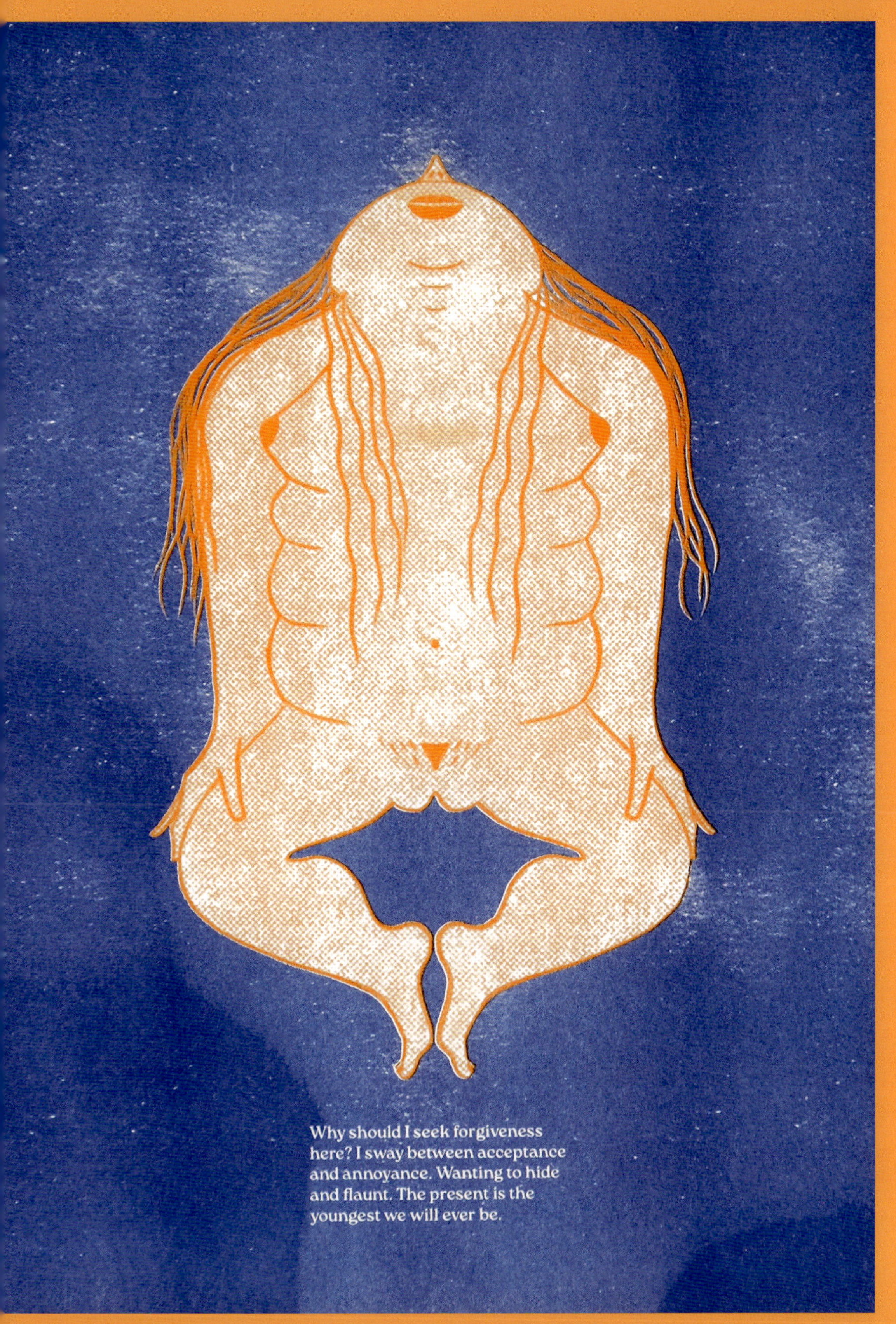

Why should I seek forgiveness here? I sway between acceptance and annoyance. Wanting to hide and flaunt. The present is the youngest we will ever be.

# "['Pretty ugly' means] perfectly imperfect."

☼Tim Lahan

Tim Lahan is an Oakland-based artist and illustrator whose work spans painting, drawing, and a range of commercial projects. His playful, minimal style has earned international recognition, balancing studio exploration with diverse creative collaborations.

Bent_(2024_Acrylic Gouache, Soft Pastel_280 x 380 mm).tif

Bunch_(2023_Acrylic Gouache, Soft Pastel_280 x 380 mm).tif

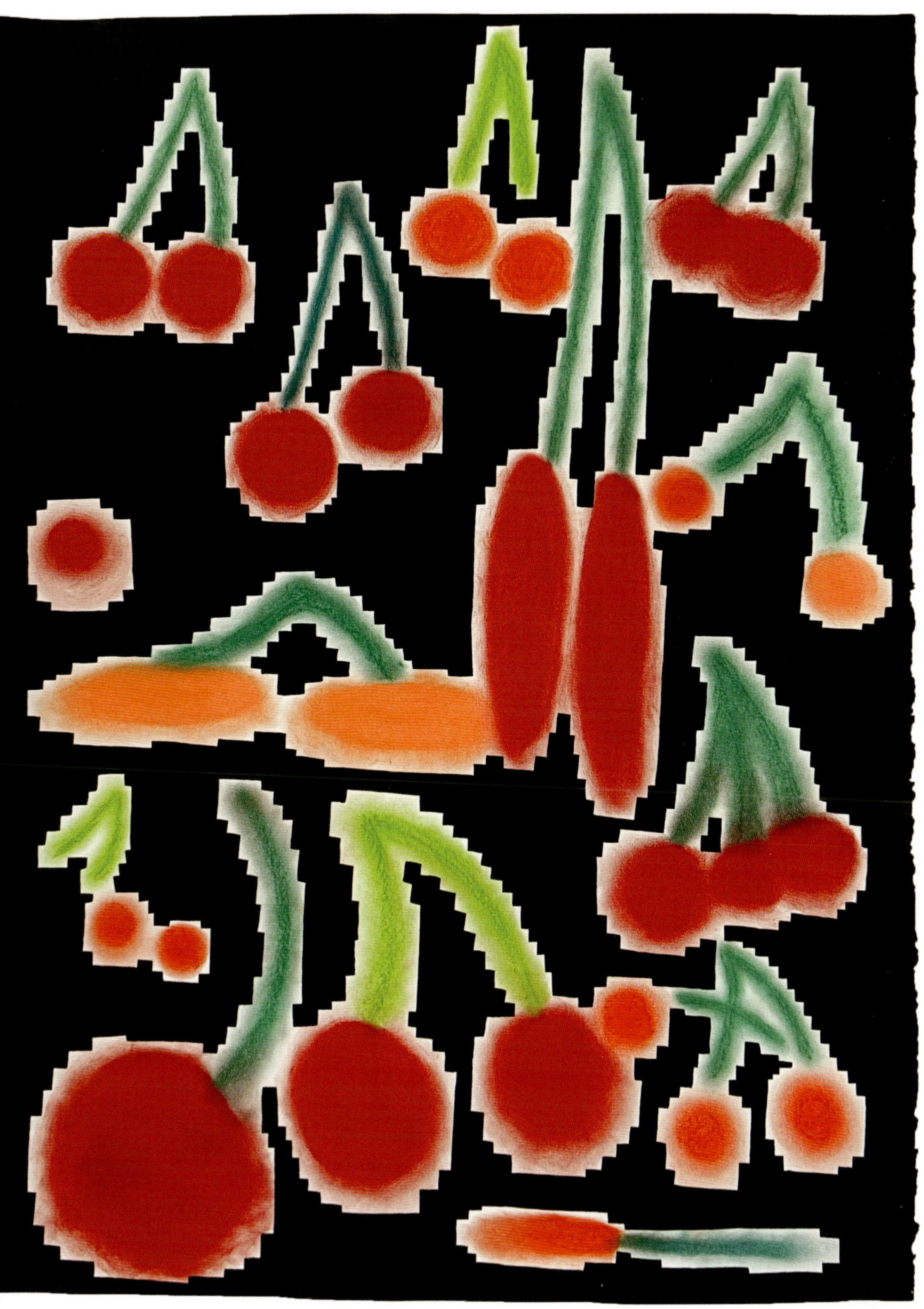

Cherries_(2023_Acrylic Gouache, Soft Pastel_600 x 760 mm).tif

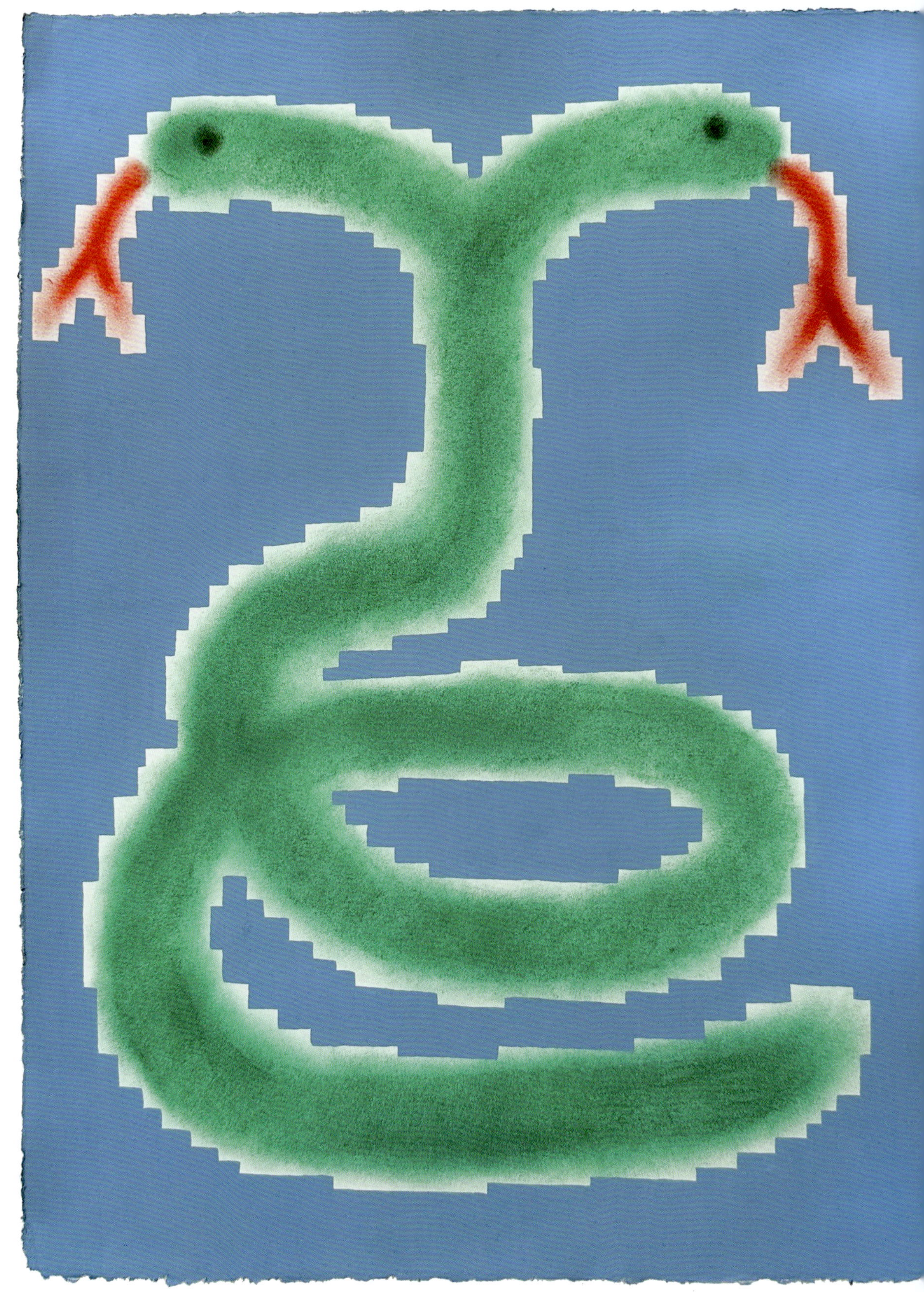



Yesterday & Tomorrow_(2024_Acrylic Gouache, Soft Pastel_280 x 380 mm).

eam_(2024_Acrylic Gouache, Soft Pastel_380 x 508 mm).tif

Horses_(2024_Acrylic Gouache, Soft Pastel_280 x 380 mm).tif

Faucet_(2024_Acrylic Gouache, Soft Pastel_280 x 280 mm).tif

Clock_(2023_Acrylic Gouache, Soft Pastel_280 x 380 mm).t

Apple_(2024_Acrylic Gouache, Soft Pastel_280 x 380 mm).tif

"'Pretty ugly' comes out when you're free, honest and playful; when you embrace your imperfections, wild imagination, and personality just plainly with joy without worrying about how things should look."

Chi Park

Chi Park is a South Korean illustrator based in London. A Kingston School of Art and Royal Drawing School graduate, she documents real-life moments through sketchbooks and brings that energy into playful, imaginative studio works exploring characters and worlds shaped by both observation and creativity.

Cookie Time_(2023_Mixed Media, Paper_250 x 210 mm).jpg

Whitelands_(2024_Mixed Media, Paper_245 x 170 mm).jpg

Client: So Young Magazine

A Girl in the City_(2023_Colour Pencils, Paper_240 x 190 mm).jpg

Collection of Faces_(2025_Colour Pencils, Paper_3735 x 4552 px).jpg

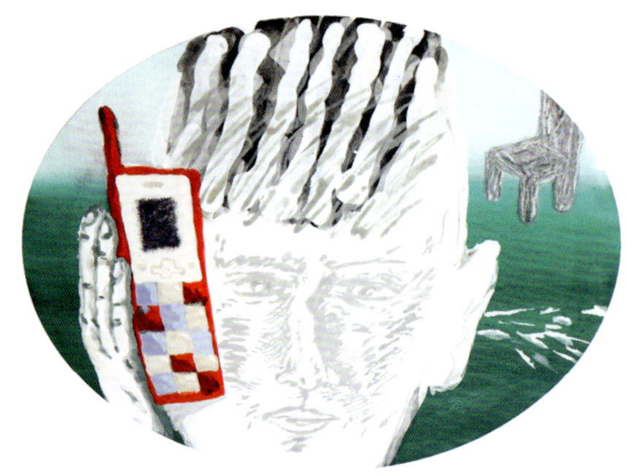

Uncommon Signals_(2025_Korean Colour, Kaolin, Canvas_400 x 500 mm).jpg

"I have two possibilities: ①On the one hand, I find an intensification of the word 'ugly'. On the other hand, the interdependence of two opposites is revealed. Both can hardly exist without each other. ②When I am preparing for the holidays, I am stressed and most of my day feels ugly—but once I fly away, everything is just pretty."

☼Luca Schenardi

Luca Schenardi is a Swiss illustrator and artist known for his editorial work in The New York Times, Bloomberg Businessweek, Die Zeit, and more. Since 2003, he has also designed LP covers and band merch for the music industry. He studied at HSLU in Lucerne and is represented by the agency Wildfox Running.

Killershrimps_(2023_Digital_261 x 611 mm).jpg

Client: Lily's Restaurant Zurich, Internal Newspaper

How To Hunt The Sasquatch_(2024_Digital_119 x 151 mm).jpg

Client: The New York Times Bookreview

The Swiss Farmer's Buffet_(2024_Digital_198.04 x 229.53 mm).jpg

Client: Swiss Energy Foundation

The Final Place, Songbook Illustration_(2024_Digital_149 x 210 mm).jpg

Clients: Cruise Ship Misery (Band), Der gesunde Menschenversand (Publisher)

'orca, Songbook Illustration_(2024_Digital_210 x 295 mm).jpg

Clients: Cruise Ship Misery (Band), Der gesunde Menschenversand (Publisher)

Compendium Of Unease, CD Cover_(2023_Digital_140 x 127 mm).jpg

Client: Just Another Foundry (Artist/Grou

A City from Scratch_(2023_Digital_2800 x 2800 px).jpg

Client: The New York Times Opinion

Public Luxury_(2024_Digital_125.02 x 188.98 mm).jpg

Client: WOZ

AI - The Ghost Out Of The Bottle (Illustration for an Essay)_(2024_Digital_210.99 x 286 mm).jpg

Client: NZZ Folio

“[‘Pretty ugly’] is something that is strikingly unconventional or imperfect, yet possesses a rough charm or beauty that resonates emotionally, challenging traditional standards of attractiveness.”

Lulu Lin

Lulu creates on her iPad using clean outlines and naturally blended colours. Her process is intuitive and emotion-led, resulting in artwork that reflects personal feelings while resonating with others. Each piece is a genuine, relatable exploration of shared emotional experiences, inviting reflection and connection.

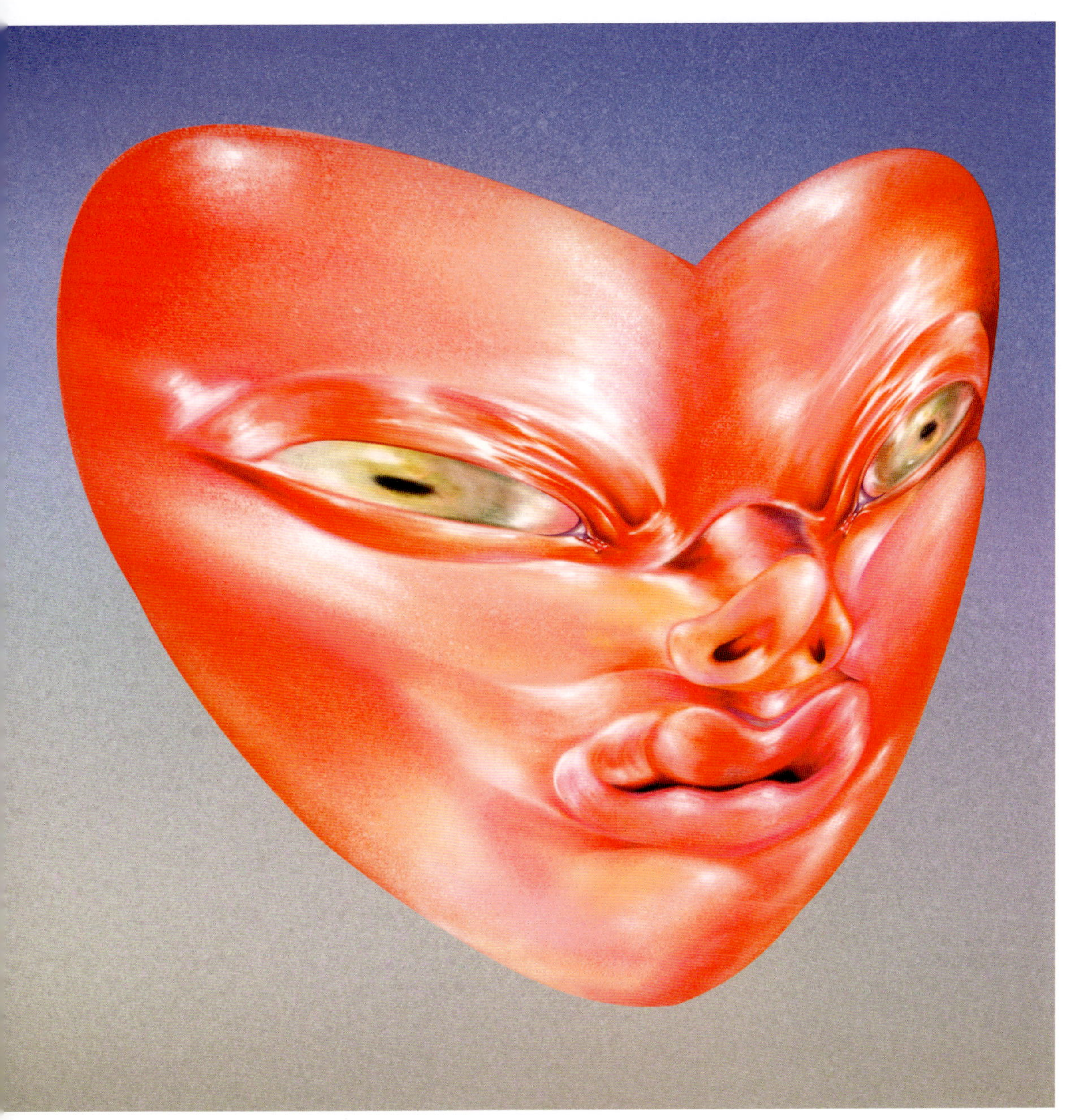

What Is Love? Baby, Don't Hurt Me. I Want To Be A Sweetheart But I Am Nothing Close To Being Cute_(2024_Digital_2000 x 2000 px).jpg

Madness Has Value_(2024_Digital_3970 x 3667 px).jpg

Illustration Modified For Sunset Rollercoaster_(2023_Oil, Digital_3508 x 2780 px).jpg

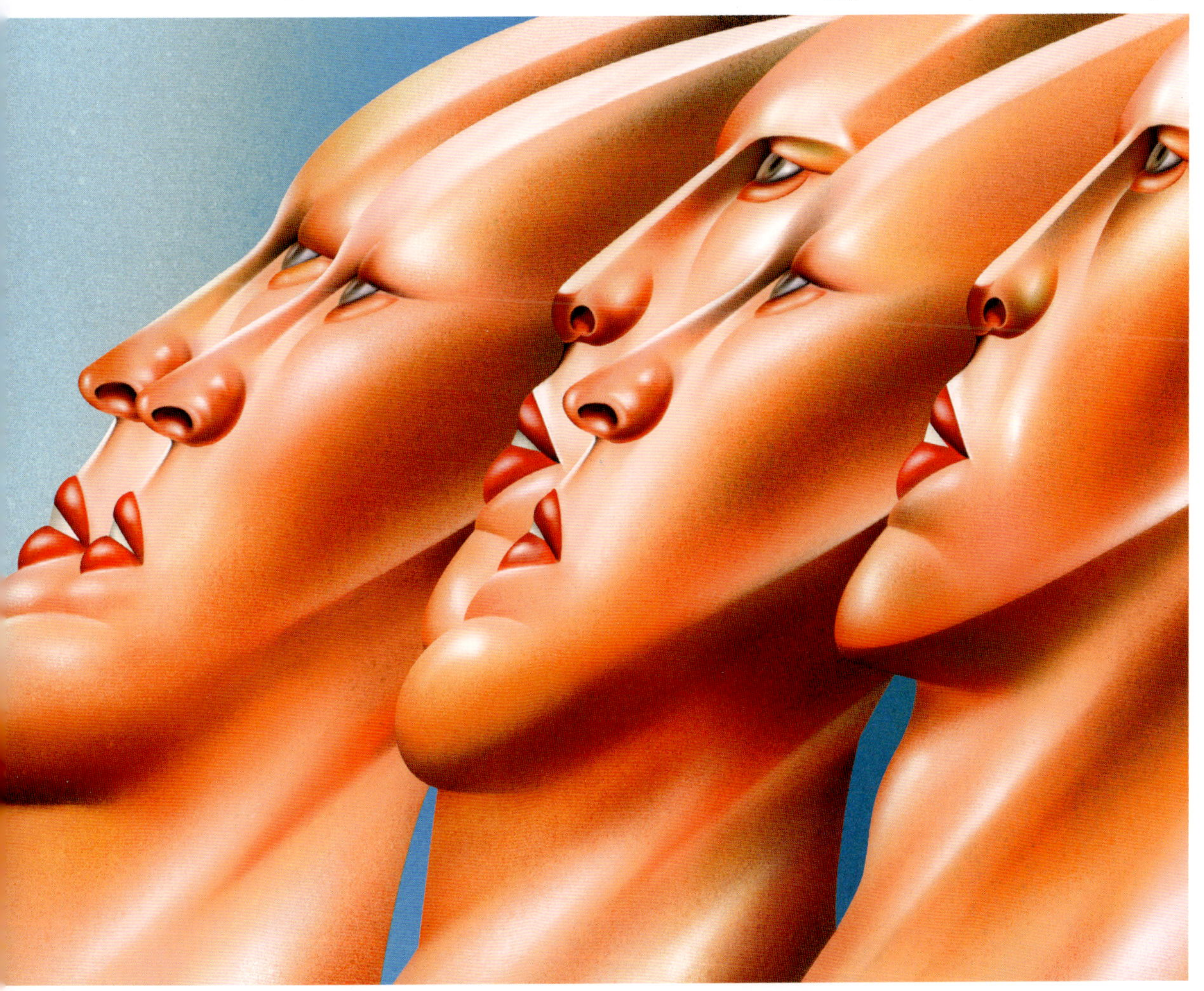

Client: Sunset Rollercoaster

(A Close Look To) What Made Me Aggressively Uneasy_(2024_Digital_1029 x 1029 px).jpg

Bye Bye My Horribly Predictable Sordid Personalities_(2022_Digital_3863 x 3296 px).jpg

I'm A Fat Flat Confused Over-Baked Hard Biscuit_(2022_Digital_3522 x 3281 px).jpg

Wholly Inadequate_(2024_Digital_1450 x 1232 px).jpg

Sensually Repulsed_(2024_Digital_3200 x 3194 px).jpg

My Inner Baby_(2024_Digital_3566 x 3084 px).jpg

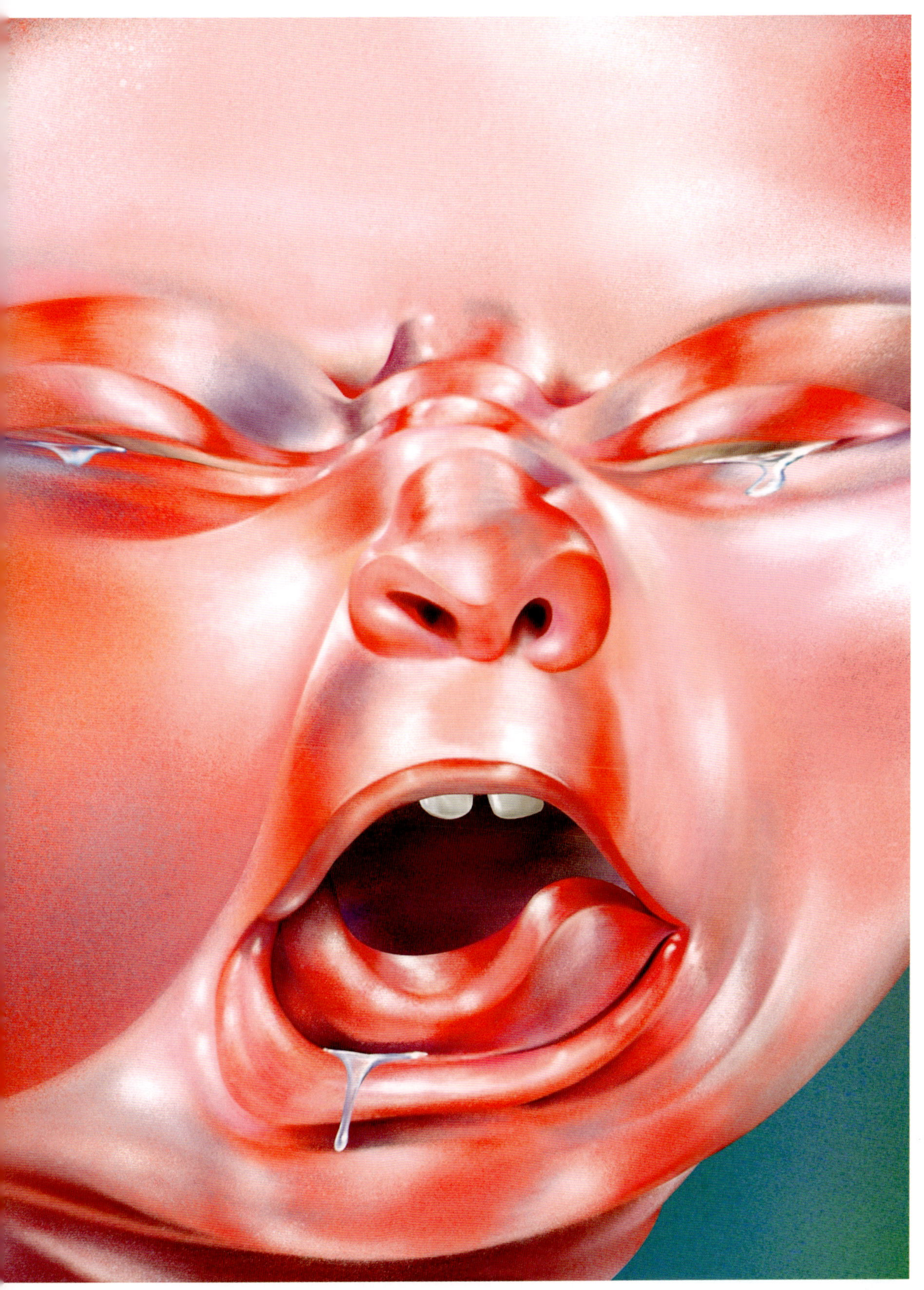

"Sometimes, the prettiness in others' eyes might be ugly to me, but the prettiness from my perspective might be the ugliness in others' eyes. Also, things that seem normal might actually be abnormal. I think 'pretty ugly' states the huge differences between people and their perspectives."

Vivienne Shao

Vivienne Shao is a Guangzhou-born, UK-based illustrator whose vibrant, comic-inspired work celebrates diverse bodies and playful narratives. Blending Chinese aesthetics with retro hues and speckled textures, her whimsical characters radiate energy and curiosity, balancing the weird, wonderful, and provocative.

Busty Cow Vol.2_(2020_Digital_210 x 297 mm).tif

C IT. SWALLOW IT. SORT IT._(2020_Digital_210 x 297 mm).jpg

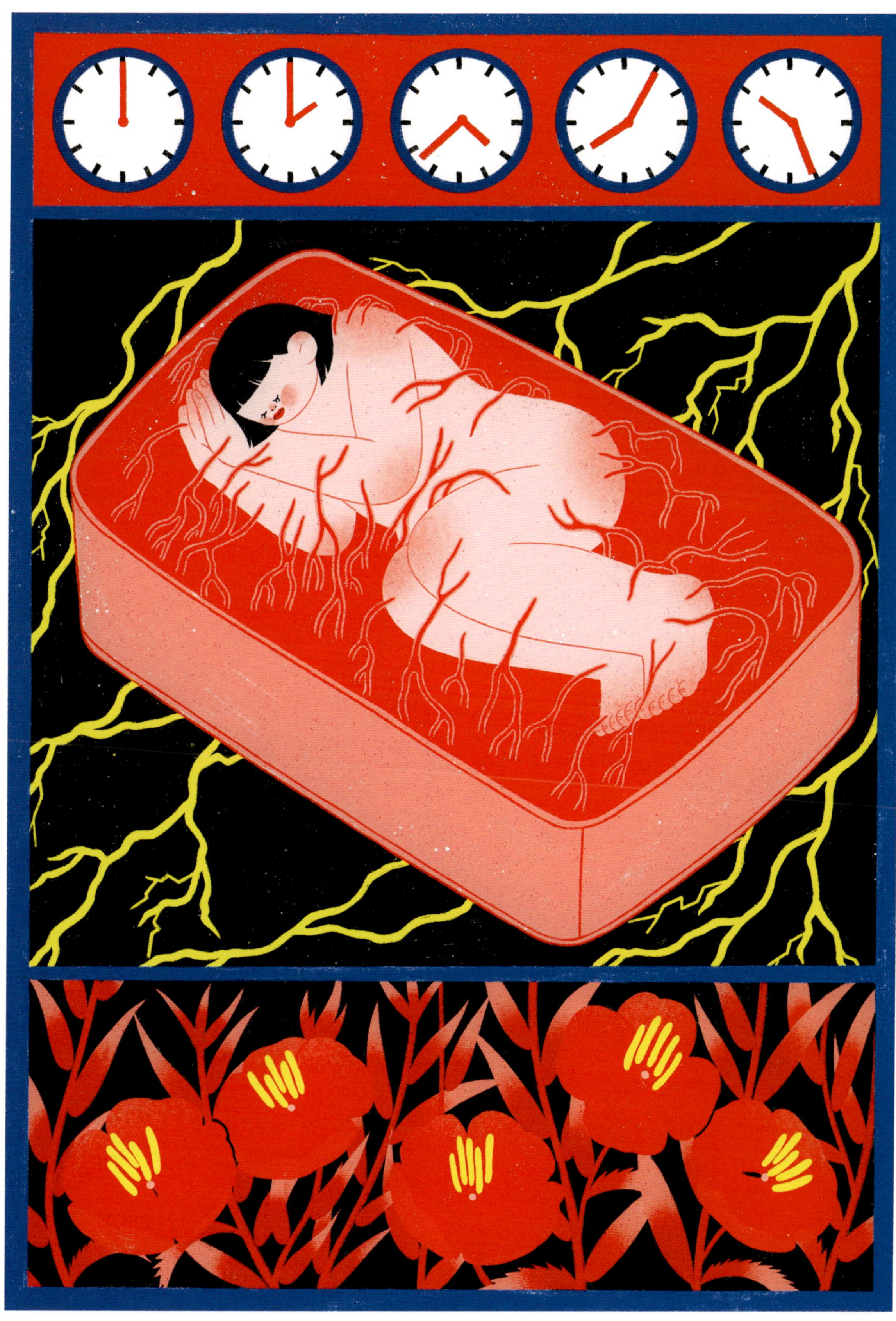

The Blood Mattress_(2020_Digital_210 x 297 mm).jpg

Gorilla Booba Gun Vol.1_(2021_Digital_210 x 297 mm).j

F*CK U_(2023_Digital_210 x 297 mm).jpg

Gorilla Booba Gun Vol.1_(2021_Digital_324 x 297 mm).jpg

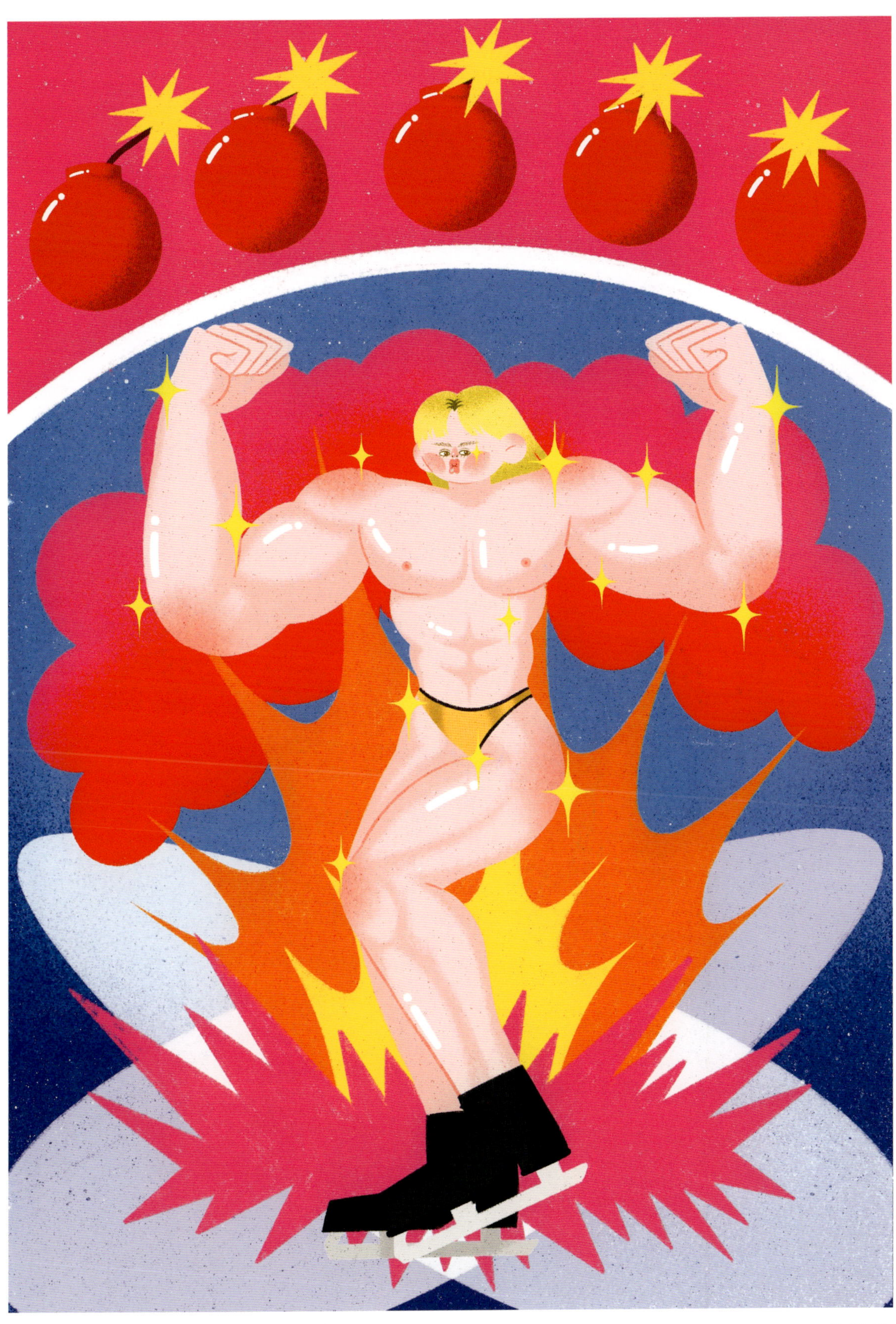

Sex Bomb_(2022_Digital_210 x 297 mm).jpg

Spotlight
special
feature

@chi_meatrui

# R u i P u

is a Chinese illustrator and designer who studied in London. His vibrant work blends printmaking textures and photo collages, often inspired by pop and meme culture. He views creation as a way to observe, highlighting interconnected stories from online communities. His clients include Nike, Spotify, and The New York Times.

Q  A

Could you share a little bit about your background/journey so far with our readers? How has your creative expression evolved over the years until you arrived at your current aesthetic/artistic style and medium(s) you work with?

I'm Rui Pu, currently living and working in China. During my undergraduate studies, I didn't receive formal education in art and design—the programme was more focused on science and engineering, which I wasn't particularly interested in. Instead, I fell in love with illustration and graphic design, so I started teaching myself.

A few years ago, I completed an MA in Illustration at Camberwell College of Arts. In the beginning, I experimented with many different techniques and mediums, such as 2D, 3D, printmaking, watercolour, creative coding, and collage. The turning point came in the second half of my time in London, when I became fascinated with internet subcultures and meme culture. I started exploring ways to connect these ideas with my work. Also, influenced by postmodern concepts like pastiche and parody, I began mixing memes collected from online communities into my paintings. These helped me develop my visual style.

A

How would you personally define the term "Pretty Ugly"?

A raw, emotional visual style that resists standardisation and rigid systems.

A

If your art could communicate one universal truth or idea about the human experience, what would it be?

Maybe that sounds a bit too grand, haha. Honestly, I just want my work to bring a bit of joy to whoever sees it—even if it's just for one second. I just asked ChatGPT the same question, and it said that maybe "pretty" and "ugly" don't have to be opposites.

A

What emotions or reactions do you hope to evoke in viewers who encounter your work? How do you approach criticism or misunderstandings, especially when challenging aesthetic norms?

I hope people see my work the way they look at memes—light and easy. I don't want to add too much metaphor or some big, serious narrative. That kind of stuff can be overwhelming sometimes. I just want people to feel happy, or maybe even laugh for a second when they see my images. The world is already serious enough.

Luckily, I haven't received any criticism or misunderstanding so far. It seems like people actually feel happy when they look at my work, and that makes me really glad.

A

How do you see the "pretty ugly" aesthetic evolving in the future, and what impact could it have on our world on a broader scale?

Challenging traditional order isn't just about visual style; it's also about the methods and mindset behind the work.

Why do you think society is increasingly drawn to unconventional aesthetics and what does it say about our culture?

Personally, I think it has a lot to do with how super boring the world has become. Everything feels the same. We're in a big "McDonaldised" society—where everything is predictable and standardised: pre-cooked meals, templated short videos, boring grid systems, and Helvetica everywhere—clean, safe, and totally unexciting. That's why non-traditional aesthetics are so appealing to me. They feel like little glitches in the system—maybe not everyone likes them, but that's exactly what makes them interesting!

What advice would you give to emerging artists who want to break away from conventional beauty standards in their work? How can they stay truly authentic when surrounded by noise?

Just do it! (Quoted from Nike)

Art of Living_(2021_Digital_6200 x 4400 px).jpg

Client: Selfridges

HuHuHu_(2021_Digital_5055 x 3780 px).jpg

Jing_(2021_Digital_3307 x 2339 px).jpg

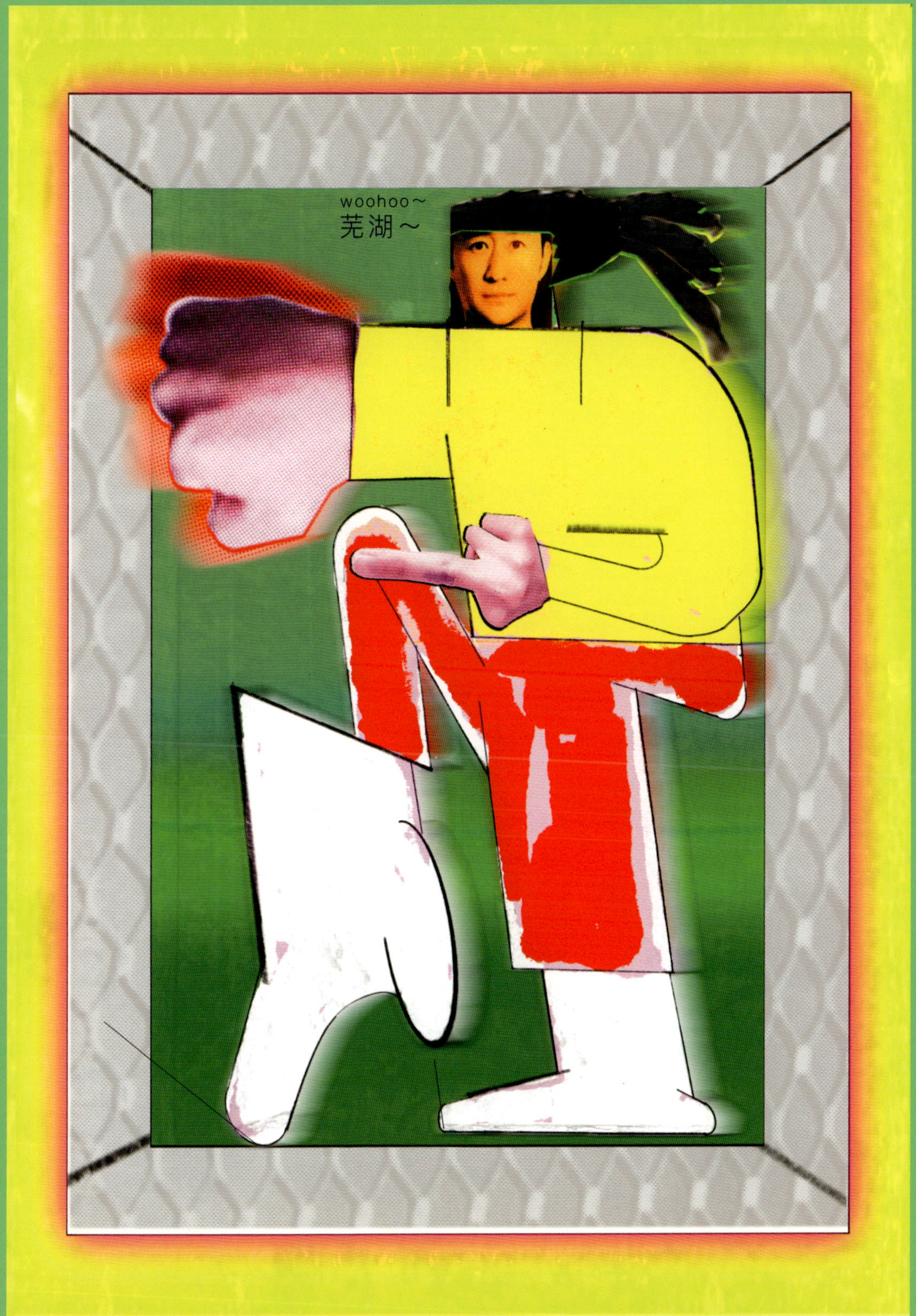

Client: It's Nice That

Mouth Map_(2024_Digital_3364 x 2320 px).tif

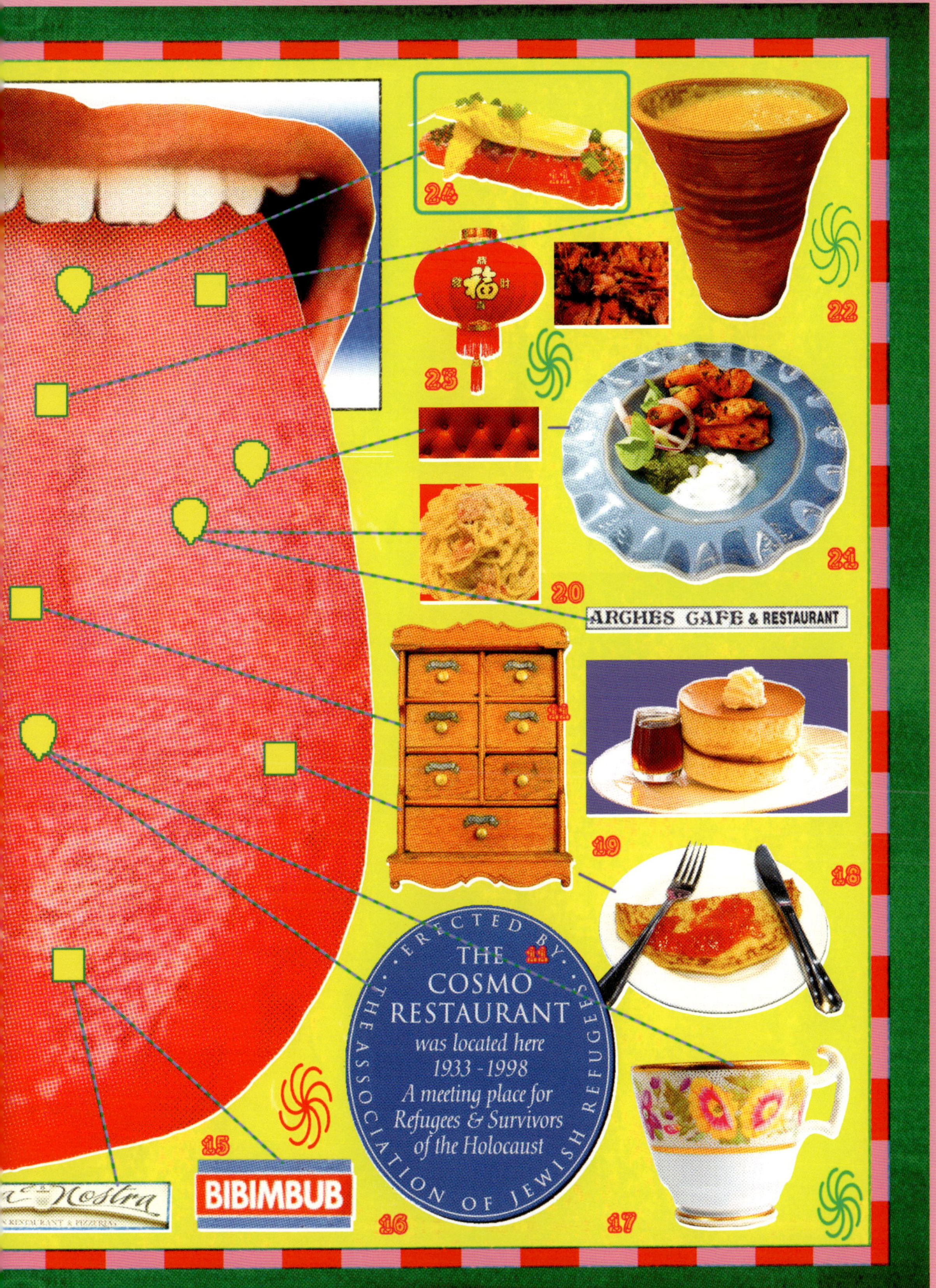
24
22
25
21
20
ARCHES CAFE & RESTAURANT
19
18
ERECTED BY THE ASSOCIATION OF JEWISH REFUGEES
THE COSMO RESTAURANT
was located here
1933 - 1998
A meeting place for
Refugees & Survivors
of the Holocaust
15
BIBIMBUB
16
17

QiaQiaQia_(2021_Digital_3527 x 2521 px).jpg

WaWaWa_(2021_Digital_3728 x 2682 px).jpg

HoHoHo_(2021_Digital_1895 x 2527 px).jpg

PaPaPa_(2021_Digital_3307 x 2339 px).jpg

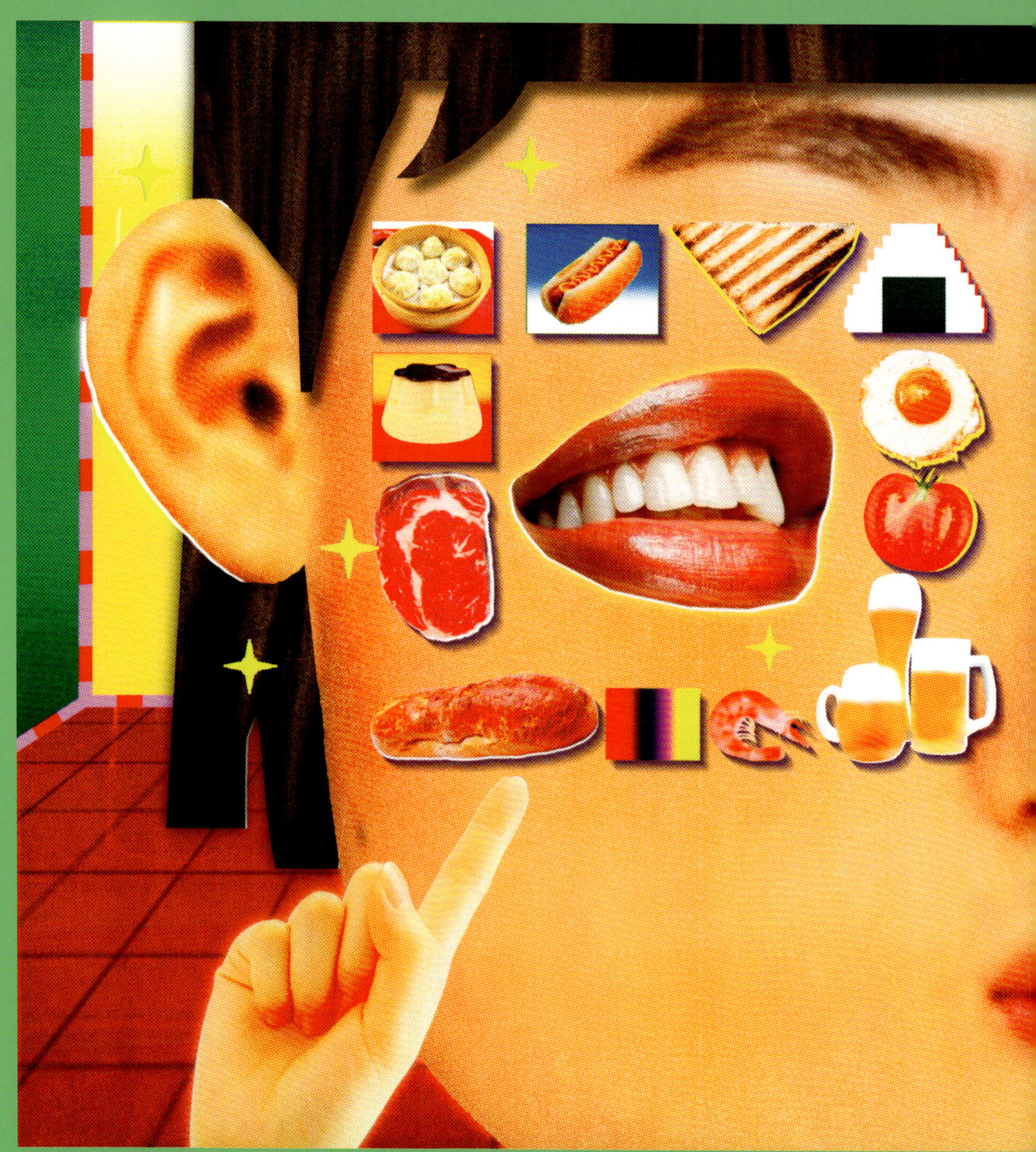

Hungry Eyes_(2024_Digital_3980 x 2000 px).tif

Client: It's Nice That

Playground_(2021_Digital_6200 x 4400 px).jpg

Client: Selfridges

SuperSelf_(2021_Digital_6200 x 4400 px).jpg

Client: Selfridges

Volcano-1_(2021_Digital_3297 x 2297 px).jpg

Volcano-2_(2021_Digital_3259 x 3137 px).jpg

The Menu_(2024_Digital_3500 x 2414 px).tif

Client: It's Nice That

“To me, ‘pretty ugly’ embodies the essence of ‘heta uma’: a Japanese term that translates to ‘bad (but) good.’ Maybe you don’t have flawless technique, but you do have taste.”

☼Haein Kim

Haein Kim is a multidisciplinary artist based in Sydney. Her practice spans across animation, illustration, and a little bit of everything else.

Summer_(2021_Colour Pencils, Paper_210 x 297 mm).jpg

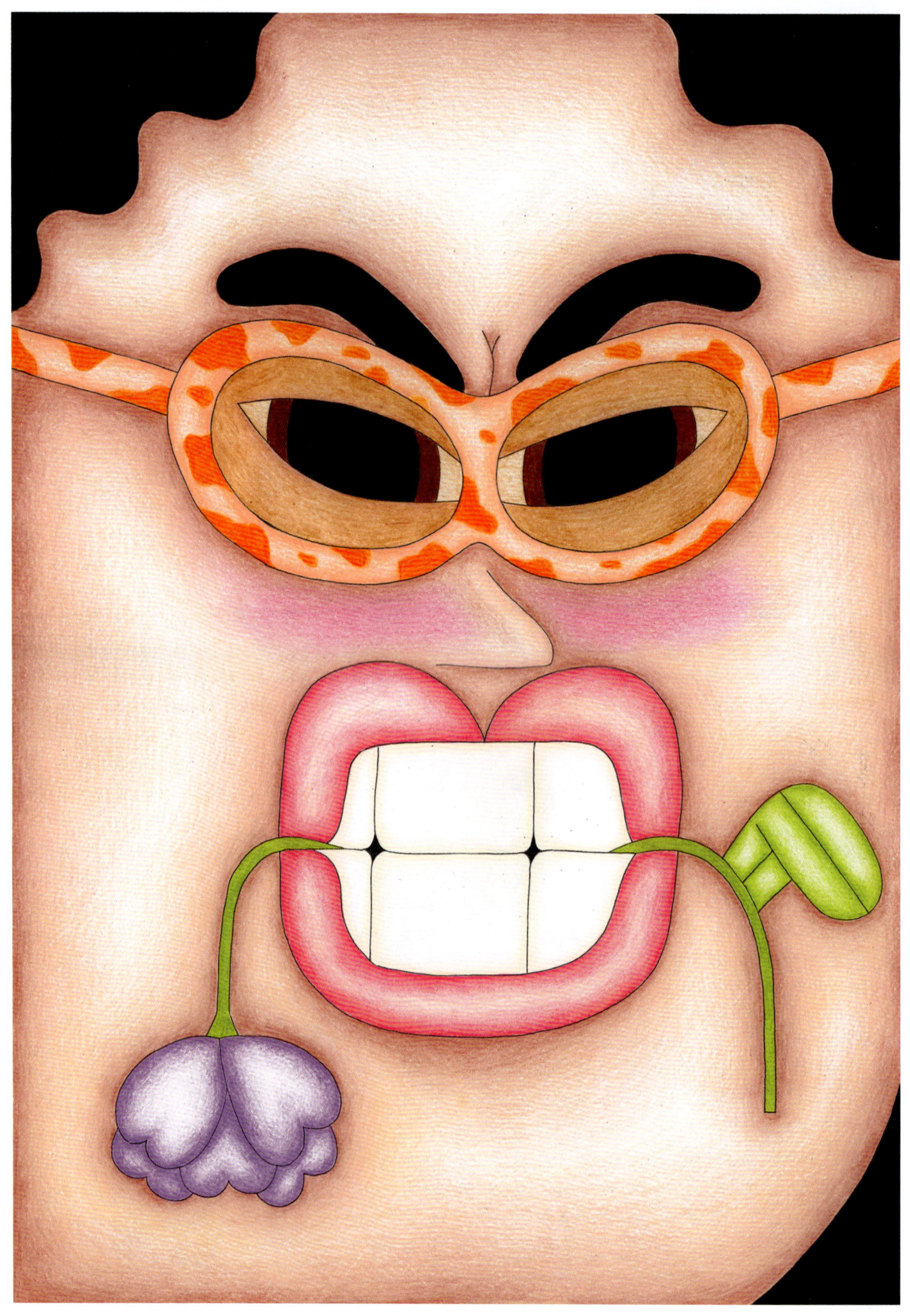

Angry Flower_(2020_Colour Pencils, Paper_297 x 420 mm).jpg

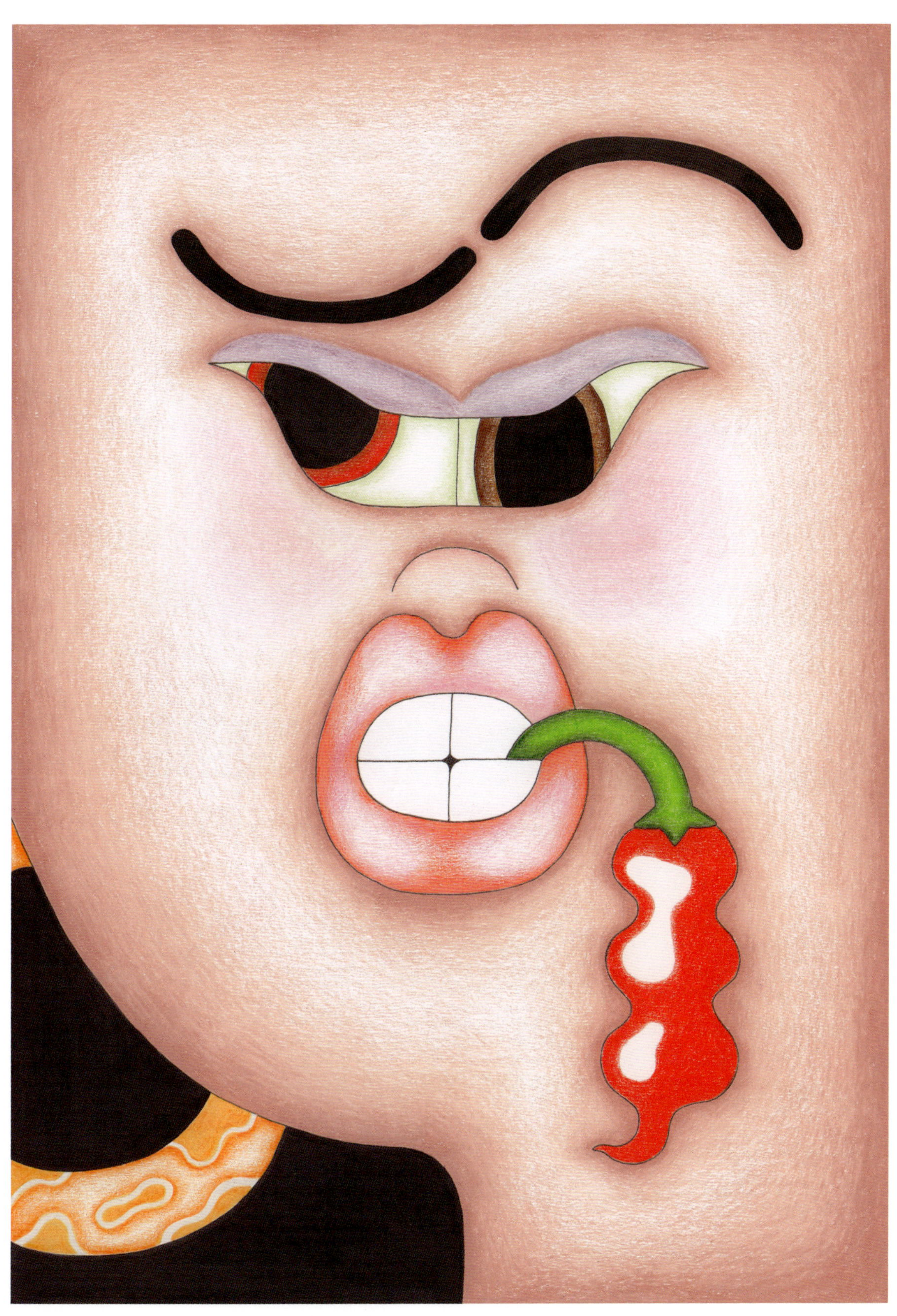

Chilli_(2021_Colour Pencils, Paper_297 x 420 mm).jpg

The Hand Of Those Who Hurt Us_(2023_Colour Pencils, Paper_297 x 420 mm).jpg

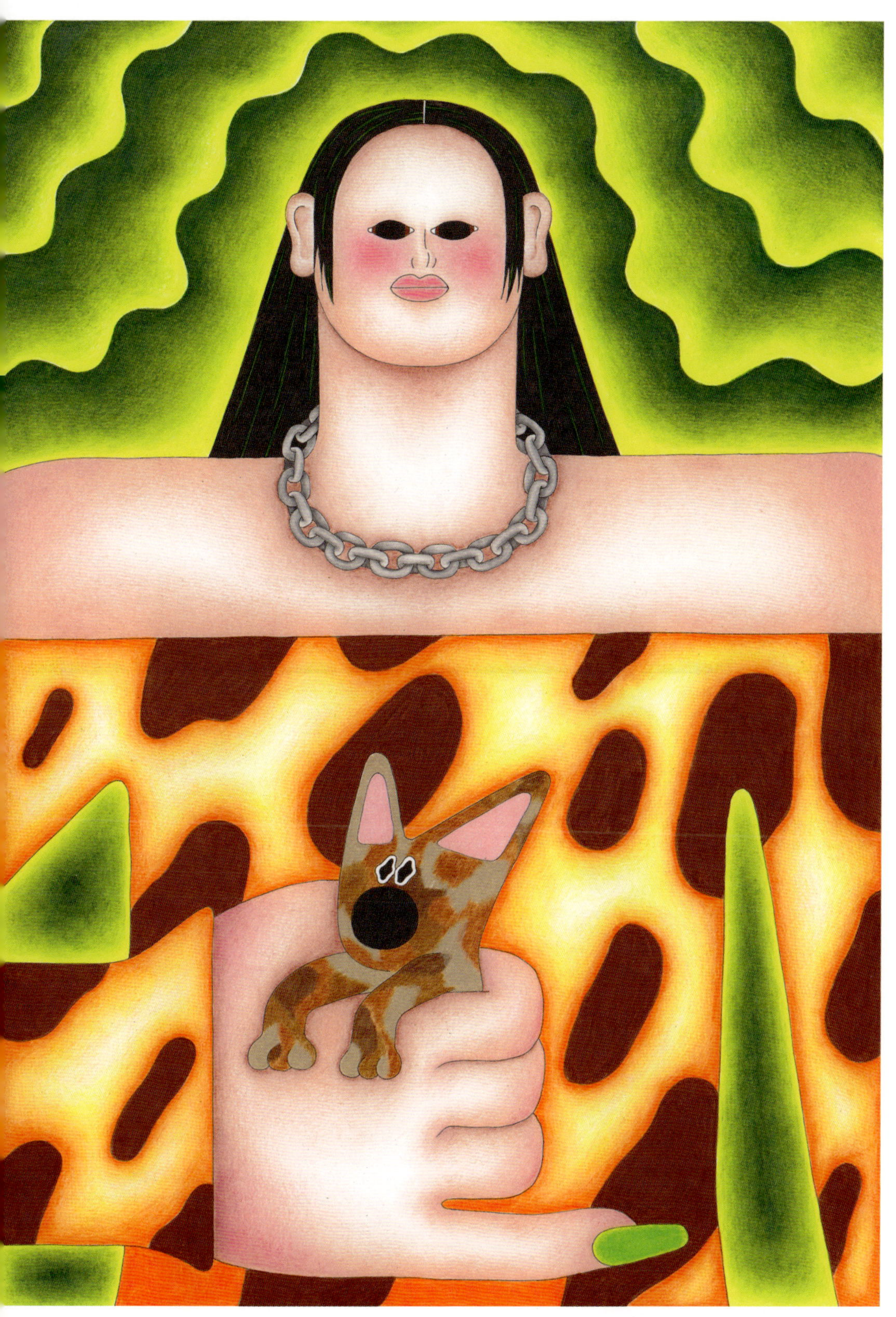

You, You Friend's Dog And Your Anxiety_(2023_Colour Pencils, Paper_297 x 420 mm).jpg

Hard Body Soft Emotions_(2023_Colour Pencils, Paper_570 x 760 mm).jpg

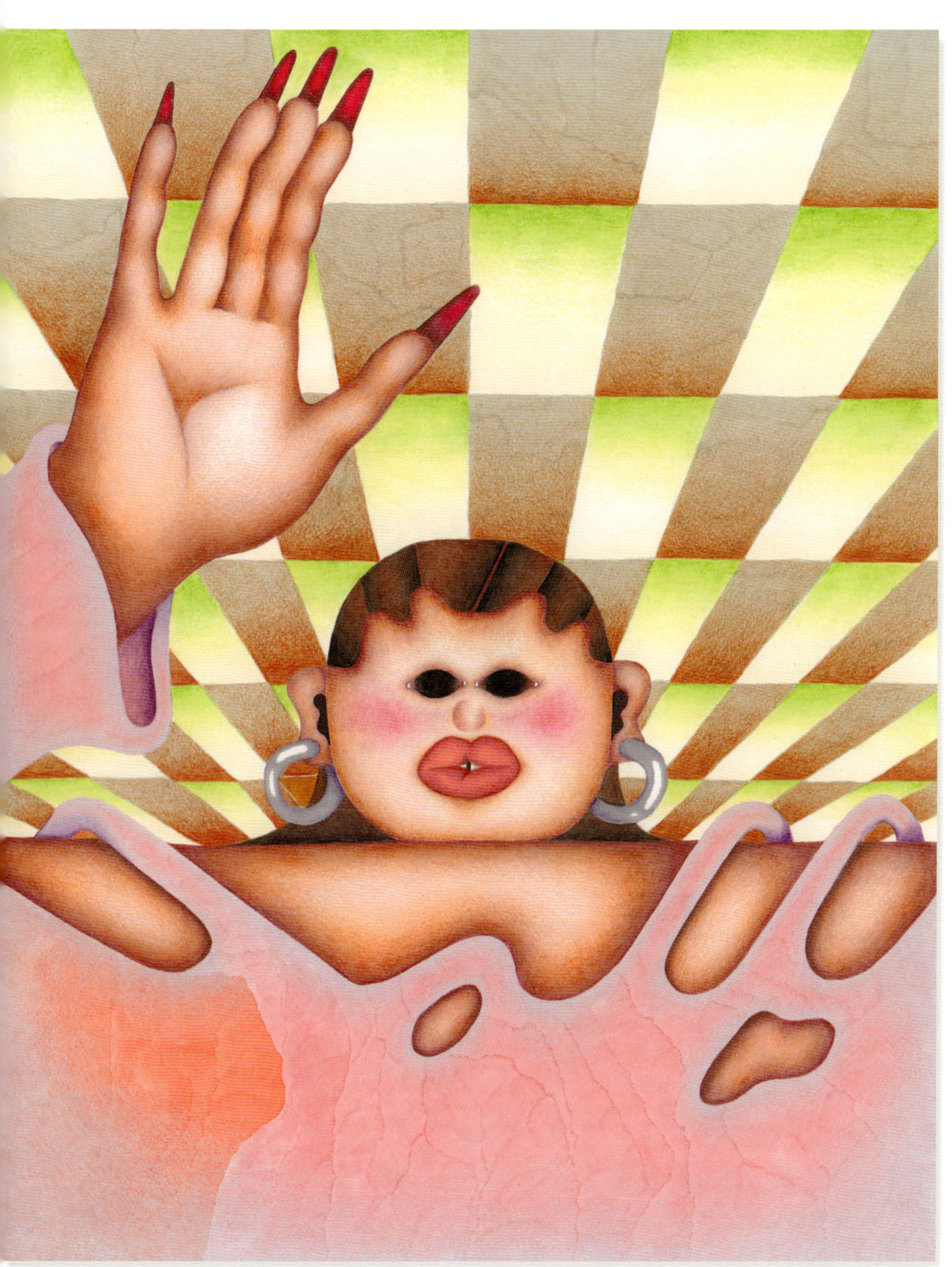

Magic Manifest_(2023_Colour Pencils, Paper_287 x 390 mm).jpg

"Perceptions of ugliness often stem from deviations from socially accepted norms, and the act of labelling something as 'ugly' is closely tied to marginalisation. That's why I'm more inspired by rethinking conventional ideas of appearance. I find joy in challenging visual norms—through distortion, reshaping, and the pursuit of the bizarre."

Talia Melda Temuçin

Talia Melda Temuçin is a freelance illustrator and artist with a background in visual communication and painting. Her wor blends delicate textures with expressive compositions, often inspired by nature and identity. She explores emotion throug subtle visual storytelling, resulting in introspective and richly layered illustrations.

Do I Really Want To Eat There Or Do I Want To Post The Meal On Instagram?_
2022_Digital_656 x 928 mm).jpg

Your Fortune? Lays On The Ground Of Your Coffee Cup_(2022_Digital_631 x 782 mm).jpg

Augmented Reality_(2022_Digital_656 x 928 mm).jpg

Garage Fitness_(2021_Digital_875 x 855 mm).jpg

Fitness Influencers Preparing For The Next Tiktok_(2022_Digital_875 x 1237 mm).jpg

Excavator Tub_(2021_Digital_656 x 928mm).jp

BVG Fun_(2021_Digital_1080 x 1320 mm).jpg

Skillful Ways To Bypass A Tricky Defense_(2021_Digital_620 x 719 mm).jpg

Bones And Slippers_(2022_Digital_874 x 1237 mm).jpg

“[‘Pretty ugly’] describes the vulnerable place where beings behave according to their true nature.”

Aris Moore

Aris Moore is an artist based in Portsmouth, New Hampshire. Her drawings explore contradictions—awkward yet familiar, strong yet vulnerable. Frequently seen sketching in cafés, her work has been exhibited across the United States and featured in New American Paintings and The Creative Block. Outside her practice, she enjoys life with her twins, August and Owen, and their cat, Theo.

Night Moves_(2024_Pencil, Coloured Pencils, Marker, Pen, Paper_114.3 × 177.8 mm).jpg

At The Park_(2024_Pencil, Coloured Pencils, Marker, Pen, Paper_215.9 × 279.4 mm).jpg

Who Are You?_(2024_Pencil, Coloured Pencils, Marker, Pen, Paper_114.3 × 177.8 mm).jpg

A Package Deal_(2024_Pencil, Coloured Pencils, Marker, Pen, Paper_114.3 × 177.8 mm).jpg

Wonder_(2024_Pencil, Coloured Pencils, Marker, Pen, Paper_114.3 × 177.8 mm).jı

Blue Trees_(2023_Pencil, Coloured Pencils, Marker, Pen, Paper_292.1 × 355.6 mm).jpg

Night Visitors_(2024_Pencil, Coloured Pencils, Marker, Pen, Paper_203.2 × 292.1 mm).jpg

"'Pretty ugly' is a mix of the grotesque and the sexy, something you love and hate at the same time, captivating in its imperfections."

Giorgia Rachel Donnan

Giorgia Rachel Donnan is a Venice-based artist and fashion design student at IUAV. Her multidisciplinary work spans drawing, photography, and painting, exploring suburban cultures through grotesque yet seductive imagery. Influenced by B-horror aesthetics, she blends distorted urban landscapes with deformed figures and vivid colour to craft unsettling yet captivating visual narratives.

Untitled Drawing For “Materia Degenere 3”_
(2023_Graphite, Paper_297 x 420 mm).jpg

Client: Diabolo Edizioni

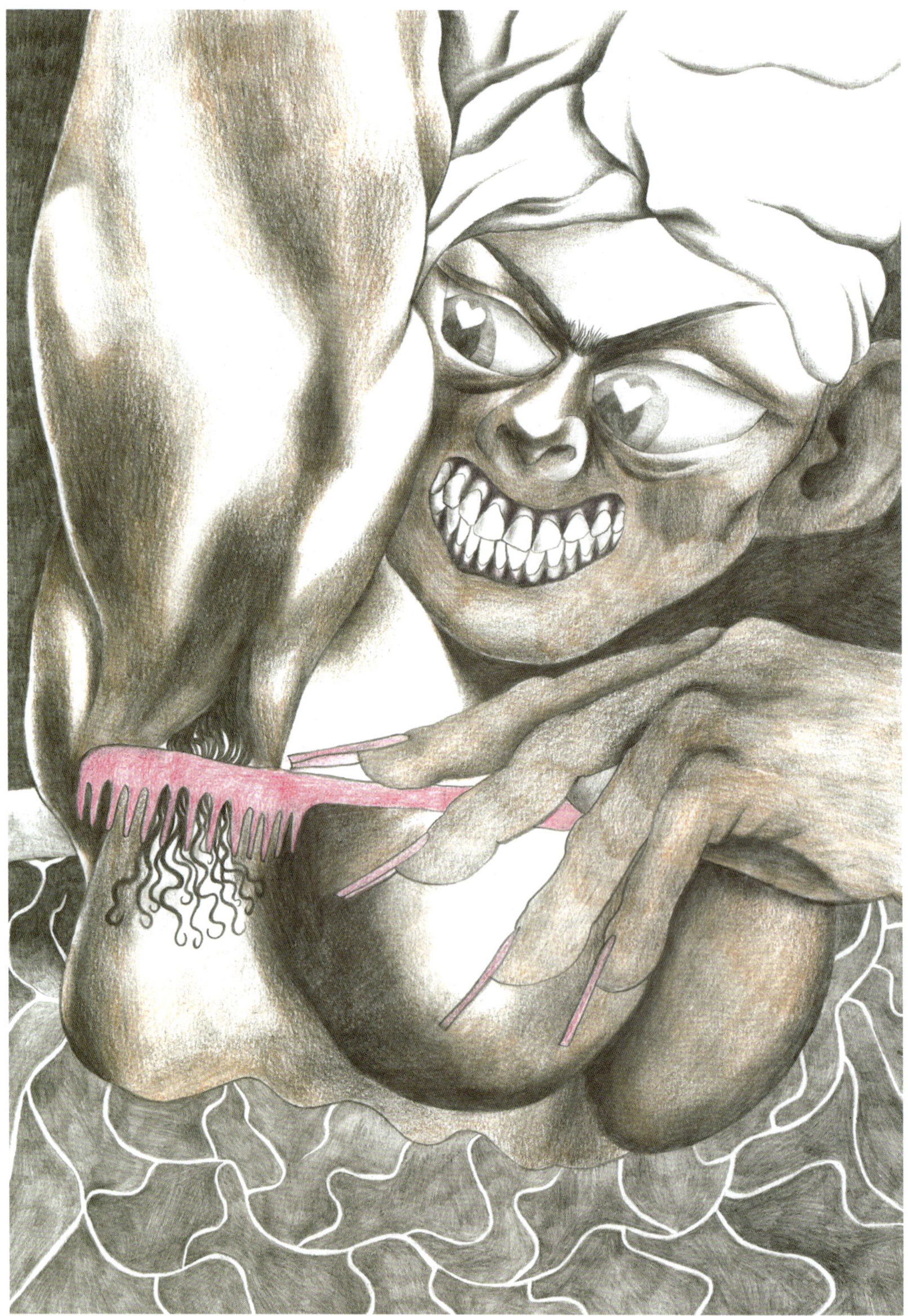

Untitled Drawing For "Materia Degenere 3"_
(2023_Graphite, Paper_297 x 420 mm).jpg

Client: Diabolo Edizioni

Untitled Drawing For "Materia Degenere 3"_
(2023_Graphite, Paper_297 x 420 mm).jpg

Client: Diabolo Edizioni

Untitled (2023_Graphite, Paper_297 x 420 mm)

Client: SPRINT

Untitled_(2023_Graphite, Paper_297 x 420 mm).jpg

Client: Wobby.club

"'Pretty ugly' resonates with me, as I enjoy exploring the line between good and bad taste. Vibrant colours and quirky characters bring my monsters to life, blending the familiar with the strange. My monsters are not just frightening—they are universal and friendly in their own way. Inspired by masks, they reflect the human imagination's endless ability to create extraordinary creatures from simple resources."

Margaux Bigou

Based in Tahiti, Margaux Bigou creates eerie, heat-soaked creatures inspired by island life. Her work spans screenprinting, risography, and delicate porcelain forms, evoking melancholy and solitude. A graduate of ENSAD Paris, she exhibits internationally and is currently developing her first graphic novel.

Hell No_(2020_Gouache, Wood_145 x 210 mm).jpg

Rodeo_(2020_Gouache, Wood_145 x 210 mm

Peace_(2021_Gouache, Wood_145 x 210 mm).jpg

Le Soleil_(2020_Gouache, Wood_145 x 210 mm).jpg

Le Mat_(2022_Gouache, Wood_145 x 210 mm).jpg

You Suck_(2020_Gouache, Wood_145 x 210 mm).jpg

Jérémiades_(2022_Risograph Printing_240 x 180 mm)

Feelings/Fillings_(2022–2023_Risograph Printing_187 x 275 mm).jpg

Screenprinting: Shlag Lab, France

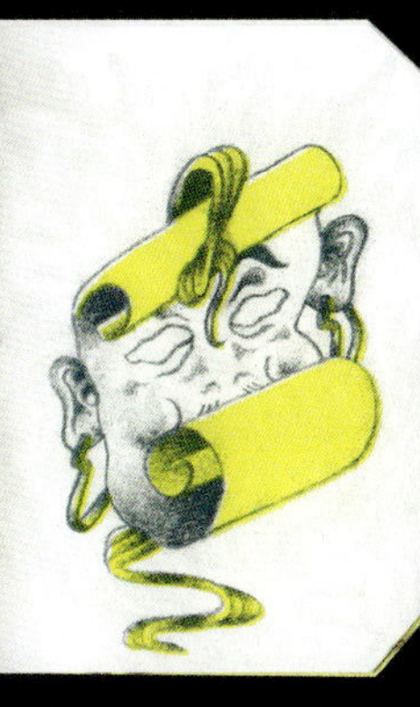

WHY

"['Pretty ugly' is] a description to place something on the threshold between the everchanging ideas of beauty and ugliness, where it simultaneously conforms, questions and joins these ideas."

※Matthias Kinnigkeit

Matthias Kinnigkeit is a self-taught visual artist and illustrator. He has worked freelance for about a decade and is currently based in Nuremberg.

Feet On The Table_(2022_Digital_339 x 339 mm).tiff

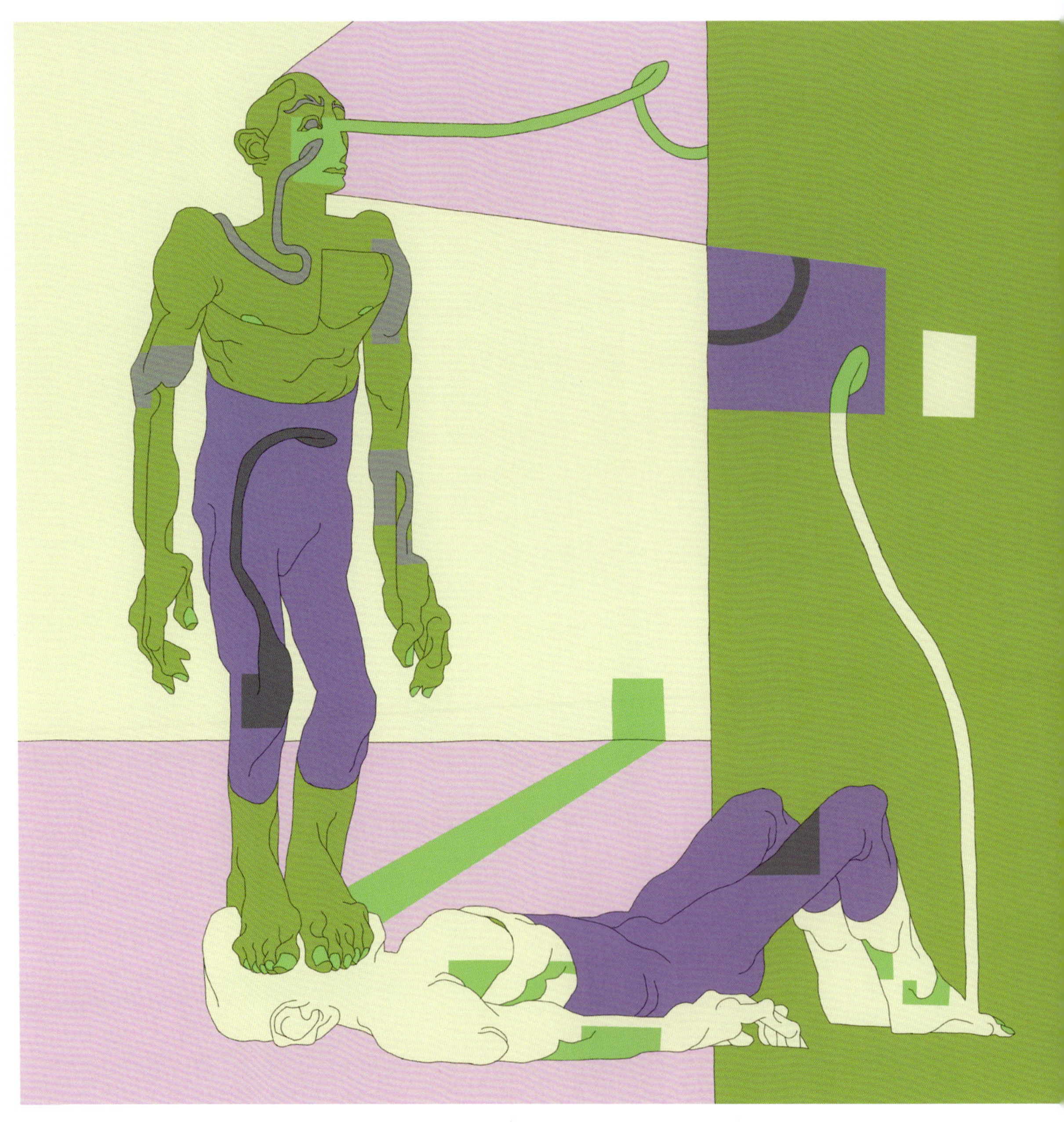

Person Standing On Another Persons Face_(2022_Digital_339 x 339 mm).tiff

Abstract Still Life With Bialetti_(2022_Digital_339 x 339 mm).tiff

Handing The Fork_(2025_Digital_191 x 269 mm).tiff

Group In Abstract Landscape_(2023_Digital_318 x 222 mm).tiff

Reading Person With Fish_(2024_Digital_381 x 303 mm).tiff

Reading Person With Dog_(2024_Digital_318 x 449 mm).tiff

“The ‘pretty ugly’ aesthetic, for me, is the fascination with imperfection. It’s that feeling of curiosity toward something we can’t quite classify, something ambiguous. It’s something against common tastes and balanced between pleasure and discomfort.”

Nick Öhlo

Nick Öhlo is an Italian illustrator and graphic designer based in Marseille. Inspired by 90s pop culture and his own experiences, he reimagines daily life with vibrant colours and quirky characters. His work blends tenderness with mischief, often rooted in nature. Averse to cold offices, he embraces creativity outdoors and under the sun.

Mrs BB_(2024_Digital_2500 × 2500 px).jpg

Stresssssssss_(2024_Digital_2480 × 3508 px).jpg

Tutti Felici_(2024_Digital_2500 × 2500 px).jpg

FK LF_(2024_Digital_2480 × 3508 px).jpg

Flowers Are Beautiful_(2024_Digital_2480 × 3508 px)

NICK ÖHLO

3LF_(2024_Digital_4648 × 4648 px).jpg

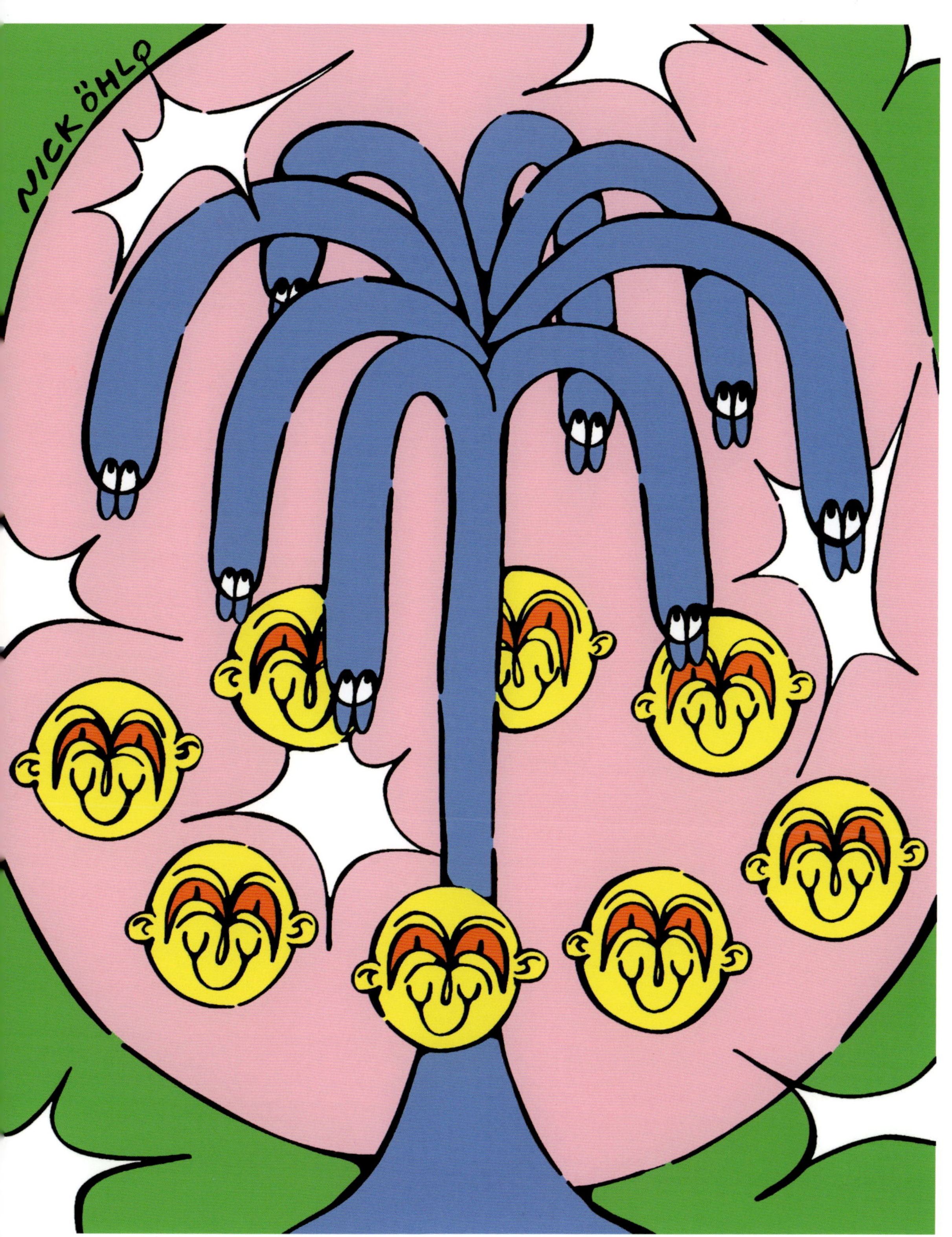


Tree Of Life_(2024_Digital_4500 × 5625 px).jpg

"['Pretty ugly' is] subverting the normative exclusionary and oppressive standards attached to the word 'beauty' and highlighting the beauty of everything normative standards deem 'ugly'."

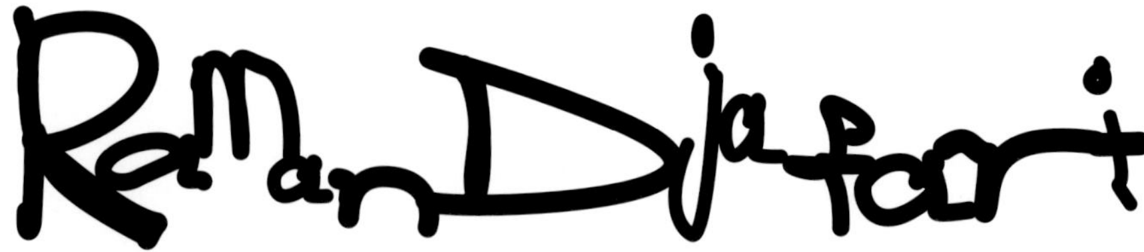

Raman Djafari

Raman Djafari is a Berlin-based illustrator, animator, and filmmaker known for blending 2D and 3D techniques. Their wor explores surreal, emotional worlds that bridge the real and fantastical. Raman has directed videos for artists like Elton Joh and Coldplay, and collaborated with clients including Adult Swim and The New Yorker. They are represented by BlinkInk i London.

V_(2023_Digital_4000 x 5000 px).jpg

3 Heads / They're Mean_(2024_Digital_4644 x 5805 px).jpg

ient: Bavarian State Opera
gency: Bureau Borsche

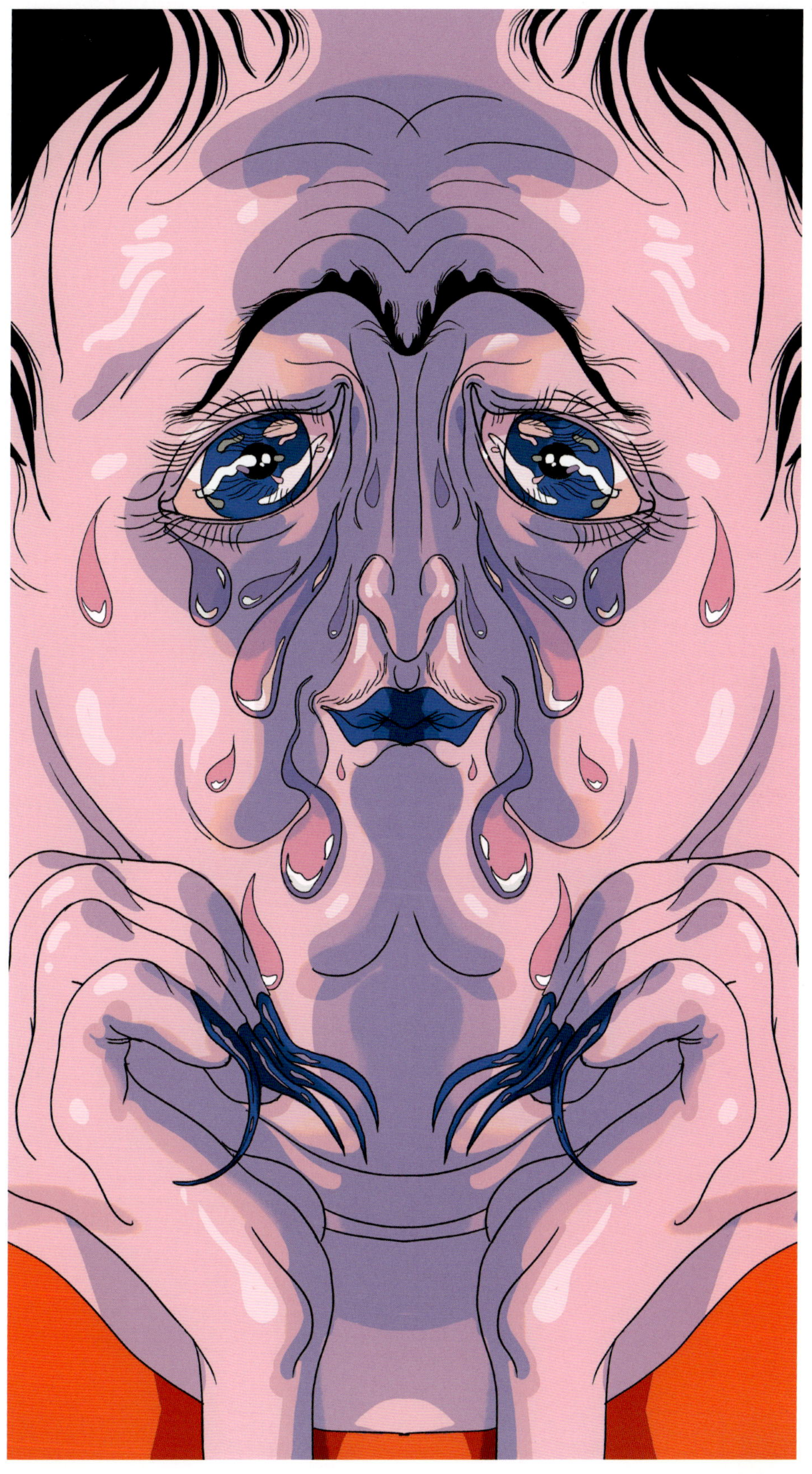

Crying_(2023_Digital_3240 x 5760 px).jpg

Clients: IF festival, Kiblind Magazine

If I Was A Moth, Would You Still Love Me?_(2023_Digital_9449 x 14173 px).jpg

Orange, Sexy, Haunted_(2023_Digital_6681 x 8351 px).jpg

Client: Global Illustration Exhibition, Seoul

Client: Kiblind Magazine

Wish You Were Here_(2022_Digital_4200 x 5250 px).jpg

Dreamers_(2024_Digital_6500 x 9750 px).jpg

Client: Anima Fest Brussels

"'Pretty ugly' refers to something ugly and a bit creepy, with strange or scary details (like a furry character with big teeth or a landscape filled with spiders and threatening mushrooms). But at the same time, these characters have funny expressions, a friendly look, and the image is full of bright colours. This contrast makes the characters more interesting and immediately grabs attention."

Francesca Colombara

Francesca Colombara is an Italian 2D animator, illustrator, and comic artist. She co-founded CIANG Studio, creating animated music videos, commercials, and shorts. A graduate of the Academies of Brera and Bologna, her music videos have screened internationally. Her graphic novel *Panic!* was published in three languages, and she has worked with clients like Bloomberg Businessweek, TED-Ed, and Tesco.

LUCID DREAM Series_(2022–2023_Digital_297.01 x 209.97mm).tif

LUCID DREAM Series_(2022-2023_Digital_297.01 x 209.97mm).tif

Curandera_(2023_Digital_297.01 x 209.97mm).tif

Rave_(2023_Digital_297.01 x 209.97mm).tif

"Beauty to me lies in quirks and defiance. What's weird or even ugly by norm can be far more compelling than perfection. 'Pretty ugly' is about daring to be different."

## Megan Du

London-based illustrator Megan Du explores womanhood through feminism, retro aesthetics, and the occult. Her bold colours, vintage textures, and distinctive characters define her visual style. Specialising in print and editorial, she has worked with Tate Modern, The New Yorker, and Bloomberg, and has been featured in It's Nice That and Creative Boom.

Peace And Release_(2022_Digital, Risography_210 x 297 mm).jpg

Lover-3_(2024_Digital_1684 x 1322 px).jpg

Country Life_(2024_Digital_1814 x 1806 px).jpg

New Nails Done!_(2024_Digital_2048 x 2077 px).jp

Get Lost_(2024_Digital_2048 x 2048 px).jpg

Client: Ember Magazine

"I find conventional beauty standards unrealistic and disingenuous. Seeing 'pretty' ideals reflected in art and media often makes me sick and feels incredibly narrow-minded. I believe everything beautiful has an ugly, uncomfortable side, and I try to embrace this in my work. I define 'pretty ugly' as beauty that defies convention—like pumpkins, mushrooms, or frogs—blending the strange and the cute to replicate this odd, honest beauty."

**Arius Ziaee**

Arius Ziaee is an animator, illustrator, and musician based in Los Angeles. Their work blends traditional hand-drawn techniques with digital elements to craft vibrant, tactile worlds inhabited by quirky, gourd-like characters. Embracing the textures and spontaneity of analogue methods, they create a signature visual style that is rich, playful, and distinctly their own.

This Is Your Brain On Egg, This Is Your Egg On Brain_
2023_Ink, Watercolour, Alcohol Markers_215.9 x 279.4 mm).jpg

Just Looking At It_(2023_Ink, Watercolour_215.9 x 279.4 mm).jp

Various Pooperoonies_(2023_Pencil, Alcohol Markers_215.9 x 215.9 mm).jpg

Never Showering Again_(2023_Ink, Watercolour, Alcohol Markers_215.9 x 279.4 mm).jpg

Brown Fungal Fog Last Thursday_
(2023_Ink, Alcohol Markers_215.9 X 279.4 mm).jpg

Thirsty Thursday_(2021_Ink, Watercolour_215.9 x 279.4 mm).jpg

Big Wishes In The Cherry Sap Forest_(2023_Ink, Watercolour, Alcohol Markers_215.9 x 279.4 mm).jpg

Bark On The Brain, In A Major Way_(2023_Ink, Watercolour_215.9 x 279.4 mm).jpg

Home Is Where The House Is_(2024_Ink, Watercolour_215.9 x 279.4 mm).tif

# Featured artists

pp.138–145 Anu Jakobson
pp.236–243 Aris Moore
pp.294–301 Arius Ziaee
pp.026–033 Bijijoo
pp.114–121 BON
pp.130–137 Cellii Bellii
pp.164–171 Chi Park
pp.122–129 Dan Lydersen
pp.282–287 Francesca Colombara
pp.084–091 Gaetan Sahsah
pp.008–025 Gao Hang
pp.034–041 Gary Card
pp.244–249 Giorgia Rachel Donnan
pp.098–113 Gregory Jacobsen
pp.218–225 Haein Kim
pp.058–067 Lazy Bug
pp.172–181 Luca Schenardi
pp.182–191 Lulu Lin
pp.068–075 Lumps
pp.250–257 Margaux Bigou
pp.258–265 Matthias Kinnigkeit
pp.288–293 Megan Du
pp.266–273 Nick Öhlo
pp.146–155 Rachel Sender
pp.274–281 Raman Djafari
pp.200–217 Rui Pu
pp.076–083 Shinkichi Hiroshima
pp.042–049 Sophie Kuhn
pp.050–057 Steph Hope
pp.226–235 Talia Melda Temuçin
pp.156–163 Tim Lahan
pp.192–199 Vivienne Shao
pp.092–097 YONK

ACKNOWLEDGEMENTS
We would like to specially thank all the artists and illustrators who are featured in this book for their significant contribution towards its compilation. We would also like to express our deepest gratitude to our producers for their invaluable advice and assistance throughout this project, as well as the many professionals in the creative industry who were generous with their insights, feedback, and time. To those whose input was not specifically credited or mentioned here, we also truly appreciate your support.

FUTURE EDITIONS
If you wish to participate in viction:ary's future projects and publications, please send your portfolio to: we@victionary.com